WHEN IN
MADRID
The Ultimate Study-Abroad Guide

Writer: Michael Raphan

SparkNotes would also like to thank Margo Orlando for her editorial contribution to this book.

See page 224 for a list of photo credits.

Spark Publishing
A Division of Barnes & Noble
120 Fifth Avenue
New York, NY 10011
www.sparknotes.com

Library of Congress Cataloging-in-Publication Data

When in Madrid: live like a local / [Michael Raphan].
    p. cm.—(When in—)

  ISBN-13: 978-1-4114-9844-0 (pbk.)
  ISBN-10: 1-4114-9844-5 (pbk.)

  1. Madrid (Spain)—Description and travel. 2. Madrid (Spain)—Guidebooks. I. Raphan, Michael. II. Title: Madrid.

DP354.W44 2007
914.6'410483—dc22

2007029511

Please submit changes or report errors to www.sparknotes.com/errors.

Printed and bound in the United States

10   9   8   7   6   5   4   3   2   1

A NOTE FROM SPARKNOTES

Congratulations on your decision to study abroad! Living in a new country, whether for a semester, a year, or longer, will enlighten you in ways you can't even imagine. Today, many consider travel abroad to be an essential step in a young person's education. Immersing yourself in a new culture, among new people, places, and things, will not only broaden your worldview, but also better equip you to face the challenges of a rapidly globalizing future.

We created the *When In* series to help you make the most of your time abroad. This book is intended for those who have already been accepted into a study-abroad program or have made the decision to live overseas. Your college or university will advise you about choosing a program, prerequisites and academic requirements, paperwork, and financial arrangements, so our focus is on the next step: the challenges you'll face as you settle into your new life. Our goal is to give you *exactly* what you need to know to make a smooth transition and get the most out of your time abroad.

Unlike traditional travel guides, the *When In* series focuses on the basics of living daily life as a study-abroad student:

- Nuts-and-bolts information, from finding housing to setting up a bank account to getting medical care

- The inside scoop on living on a student's budget

- The city's coolest restaurants, bars, clubs, study spots, and other places to hang out with friends

- Concise information on art, theater, film, music, sporting events, and other activities to keep you busy and involved in city life

With your *When In* guide, you'll *live like a local* in no time. Good luck!

Got comments? Your feedback makes us better. Contact us at www.sparknotes.com/comments.

KEY TO SYMBOLS

We use the following symbols throughout this guide:

Ⓐ	Address
Ⓣ	Telephone number
Ⓦ	Website
Ⓜ	Metro stop

10 TIPS FOR MAKING THE MOST OF YOUR TIME ABROAD

1. *Do* make friends with the locals. This will be one of the most rewarding aspects of your stay. Now's not the time to hold back!

2. *Do* take seriously every opportunity to practice speaking a new language. Immersing yourself in the language day in and day out will speed your learning process.

3. *Don't* worry about what you're missing back home. Do your best to live in the moment and embrace this amazing opportunity.

4. *Do* take advantage of cheap flights and train fares. You'll likely have frequent breaks—or, at least, greater freedom than you're used to—and it's easy and affordable to take weekend or even weeklong trips to new places.

5. *Do* keep a journal, create a blog, snap pictures, shoot videos, or otherwise record your time abroad. You'll want to remember and share all the details.

6. *Don't* be afraid to speak up if you find yourself facing anti-Americanism or stereotypes. Remember that you can counter negative stereotypes by setting a good example abroad.

7. *Don't* let culture shock get you down. Confusion is a normal part of travel, and only by taking time to settle in and make friends will you conquer it.

8. *Do* immerse yourself in the local culture. Eat what the locals eat. Shop where they shop. If you can't find a familiar item from home, live without it.

9. *Don't* embark on your experience with assumptions or preconceptions. Your new life will surprise you in every possible way—and you should let it.

10. *Don't* view your study-abroad time as your one and only chance to experience life abroad. Relish the everyday moments and reassure yourself that you'll be back!

Other titles in the *When In* series include:

CONTENTS

INTRODUCTION

Bullfights. Sweltering heat. Flamenco dancers and women wearing lace *mantillas* (scarves). Long, late nights of bar crawls, club hops, and endless plates of *tapas* (light snacks). Madrid is a magical place that fuels the imagination—a place that prompted Hemingway to say, "Nobody goes to bed in Madrid until they have killed the night."

You may indeed find yourself eating dinner at midnight and staying out until dawn more often than you ever thought possible, and it's true that the city is rich with amazing Spanish food and tradition. However, the Madrid of the imagination pales in comparison to the Madrid of real life, where *Madrileños*—and you among them!—soak in the sun at terrace tables and fuel up for a day of school or work by tossing back a small, strong *café solo* (espresso) at a packed local bar. It's a city of tradition, but it's also a vibrant twenty-first-century European capital with a cosmopolitan attitude, and it will make an impression on you that will last a lifetime.

HISTORY

The exact circumstances surrounding the founding of Madrid remain a matter of debate. Some historians contend that the city was settled in the 800s CE by Muhammad I, a prince of Córdoba, as the city of Magerit. Others believe that the true founding occurred much earlier, when Romans built the settlement of Matrice in the second century CE on the same spot. Whichever the case, Madrid failed to thrive for several hundred years, even after Muslim rulers were driven from the country in 1110. This was primarily due to the strength of neighboring city Toledo, where wealthy landowners had concentrated their power, thus draining resources and money from Madrid.

After surviving royal political in-fighting, the Black Plague, and most of the Spanish Inquisition, Madrid finally embarked on its path to becoming a capital city when the royal power couple, Isabella and Ferdinand, sent Christopher Columbus to America in 1492. Although the city didn't reap the benefits of this until the mid-sixteenth century, it was this event that set Madrid on a new course. During this time period, Madrid's success still depended on the success of Toledo; it wasn't until riches from New World conquests started pouring in that Madrid vaulted above its rival and neighbor.

Felipe II established Madrid as a permanent capital in 1561. However, various unwise rulers during the sixteenth and seventeenth centuries—including Felipe III, Felipe IV, and Carlos II—failed to improve the lot of Madrid's citizens, despite the riches flowing to the city from expeditions in the New World. Although the royalty and aristocracy lived lavishly, they basically ignored the destitution and suffering around them.

Major internal conflicts pounded Madrid beginning in the eighteenth century. Felipe V became king of Spain in 1700, but the War of Spanish Succession soon followed after the legitimacy of his claim to the throne was questioned. He died in 1746, and his successors, Carlos III and Carlos IV, also confronted internal strife, mainly in the form of citizen revolts in the capital. In 1808, Napoleon conquered Madrid, and Spain lost its throne to France. Subsequently, the country erupted in a War of Independence against the French, which lasted five years. When Maria Cristina, the mother of the child-queen Isabel II, took the throne in 1833, Spain's conservatives rebelled, sparking a series of conflicts that lasted for decades. The 1930s saw Spain crack apart in civil war, and in 1939 General Francisco Franco conquered Madrid and the rest of Spain, beginning a long dictatorship during which Spaniards suffered seemingly endless poverty and hardship.

When Franco finally died in 1975, the country returned to democracy—and began to thrive. The Madrid of today bears little resemblance to the Madrid that Franco finally bid *adiós* to in 1975. Today's Madrileños count themselves among Europe's elite in terms of fashion, financial earning power, and quality of life. Madrid, long in the shadow of Barcelona culturally and financially, has come into its own. In many ways, the city is more powerful today than it ever was before.

CULTURE

One thing is certain: You'll have fun while you're in Madrid. The city teems with bars, restaurants, cafes, and clubs, and Madrileños know how to enjoy them. Dinner starts late, and drinking and dancing even later. It's almost expected that, on the weekends at least, you won't head home until dawn. More traditionally Spanish than cities to the north, such as Barcelona, Madrid's culture emphasizes family, tradition, and quality of life as well as fun. Families stay close—it's normal for adult children to live at home until they marry—and traditions such as the long midday meal followed by a *siesta* (nap) are still commonplace. And there's no escaping the Catholic influence: You may be shocked at the number of Catholic holidays that shut down schools and businesses.

Things move slowly in Spain, so practice your patience before you arrive. Basic tasks—such as getting Internet service hooked up or simply waiting in line at the supermarket—may take much longer than seems reasonable. It doesn't help matters that many shops close for several hours in the afternoon. The culture in many ways emphasizes family and personal life over the all-consuming, work-as-life business that Americans are used to, which can be either pleasant or enraging, depending on what you're trying to cross off your to-do list.

UNIVERSITY LIFE

Students are required by law to attend school until age sixteen. If they pass the exams leading up to this point, they earn the American equivalent of a high school diploma and the title of *graduado escolar*. Next, students can choose to enter the work force; begin vocational training known as *Formación Profesional,* which trains students to become mechanics, hairdressers, electricians, and so forth; or begin the two-year college-preparatory program known as the *Bachillerato Unificado Polivalente.*

Going to college in Spain is a far cry from going to college in the United States. Moving to campus—an American rite of passage—doesn't exist in Spain because nearly all students live at home and commute to the nearest university. There are virtually no dining halls or dormitories, and if students choose to attend a school far from home, they rent an apartment and figure out meals on their own. This is a pretty rare move, however. Young adults in Spain often rely on their parents for housing and home-cooked meals well into their thirties.

Madrid has three public universities: the Universidad Autónoma, about forty minutes north of the city center; the Universidad Complutense, Madrid's oldest university, founded in 1499; and the Universidad Carlos III, a relatively new university established in old, converted army barracks in 1970. The academic schedule is slightly different from what you might be used to. The fall semester begins in October and ends in February, while the spring semester goes from February until the end of June. There is no break between semesters, but students have three months off for summer vacation.

Classes at Madrid's universities are generally lecture-style, with little interaction between professors and students. And because professors provide a syllabus that outlines exactly what the course will cover, it's not unusual for students to skip class altogether and study independently from the assigned books. In the end, the only thing that counts is passing the final exam—a notoriously difficult task. Young Spaniards complete their university degrees in an average of seven to eight years.

LIVING ON THE CHEAP

Madrid, like any major metropolis, can be frighteningly expensive if you don't monitor your cash carefully. However, stretching your euros without cramping your style isn't an insurmountable challenge. Here are some basic tips to get you started:

- **Student ID:** As a student, you'll have access to numerous discounts all over the city, and you should always carry your student ID. Be sure to ask about student discounts whenever you buy tickets for museums, plays, films, or music or dance performances and whenever you make travel arrangements.

- **International Student ID and Exchange Cards:** An International Student Identity Card (ISIC) or International Student Exchange Card will give you discounts on hostels, restaurants, tours, clubs, and attractions in more than 100 countries, as well as access to emergency helplines, health insurance, and other benefits. Some cards also offer discounts on international phone calls, airfares, and shopping. You can get these cards in the United States, at student-travel agencies such as STA, or in Madrid at agencies such as Funiversal and TIVE. See www.isecard.com or www.isiccard.com for details. For nonstudents younger than age twenty-six, there is an International Youth Identity Card, which offers similar benefits. Visit www.istc.org to see whether you're eligible and to get information on how to apply.

- **Museums and theaters:** The Prado Museum is free on Sunday, as is the Reina Sofía, which also has free admission on Saturday afternoons. Wednesdays and Sundays are the designated discount days for most cinemas and theaters. For updated specials, pick up the *Guía del Ocio,* Madrid's weekly arts magazine, at a newsstand or look it up online (www.guiadelocio.es).

- **Eating out:** To save money while eating out, order tapas as opposed to meals from an à la carte menu, which prices each dish separately. To cut costs on beverages, ask for *agua del grifo,* or tap water, instead of bottled water. When ordering meals, the *menu del dia* (menu of the day) offers a set, reasonable price for a three-course lunch and sometimes dinner.

- **Terrace dining:** Although eating at an outside table is lovely in nice weather, restaurants add an additional fee to everything you order. Sometimes the menu prices will be completely different; other times, a percentage will be added to your bill—as much as 20 percent at some places.

- **Drinking:** If you're going out, start your night at the local neighborhood bars before you make your way to the trendy lounges and clubs, where cocktail prices go through the roof. As always, *cañas* (house beers) and wine are the cheapest drinking options.

10 BOOKS AND 10 FILMS TO CHECK OUT BEFORE YOU LEAVE

Once you make the move to Madrid, what exactly will you be in for? Only time will tell. But to get a first glimpse of the city and to get in the Spanish mood, check out these books and films, which relate to Madrid in particular and Spain in general:

BOOKS

1. *The Spy Wore Red,* Aline, Countess of Romanones
2. *The Family of Pascual Duarte,* Camilo José Cela
3. *Don Quixote,* Miguel Cervantes
4. *The Back Room,* Carmen Martín Gaite
5. *Death in the Afternoon,* Ernest Hemingway
6. *The Sun Also Rises,* Ernest Hemingway
7. *Iberia,* James Michener
8. *Spain in Our Hearts,* Pablo Neruda
9. *The Club Dumas,* Arturo Pérez-Reverte
10. *The Fencing Master,* Arturo Pérez-Reverte

FILMS

1. *The Pleasure Seekers* (1964), Jean Negulesco
2. *Women on the Verge of a Nervous Breakdown* (1988), Pedro Almodóvar
3. *Tie Me Up! Tie Me Down!* (1990), Pedro Almodóvar
4. *Thesis* (1996), Alejandro Amenábar
5. *Tierra* (1996), Julio Medem
6. *Open Your Eyes* (1997), Alejandro Amenábar
7. *All About My Mother* (1999), Pedro Almodóvar
8. *Sex and Lucia* (2001), Julio Medem
9. *The Sea Inside* (2004), Alejandro Amenábar
10. *Volver* (2006), Pedro Almodóvar

1. Paperwork & Practicalities

Your life in Madrid will surprise you in ways you can't even imagine—but you don't want any surprises that will prevent you from getting there. The first order of business is getting a passport—and if you already have one, you'll need to make sure it won't expire while you're away. You'll also need to get a student visa. Be sure to apply well in advance of when you need them, as they can take a month or more to process.

Your university will likely guide you along the way when it comes to your passport and visa applications, but we'll give you a crash course so that you know exactly what to expect. Once you've taken care of these nuts and bolts, you can get to the fun parts—like figuring out the fastest way to get from Barajas airport to your first tapas feast.

PASSPORTS

If you've never had a U.S. passport, you can apply for one in person at your local passport facility (there are 7,000 such facilities in the United States). If you're renewing your passport, apply by mail unless your most current passport has been damaged, lost, or stolen or was issued when you were younger than age sixteen. Standard processing time for passports is six weeks; expedited service, with an extra fee, takes two weeks. Most passports are valid for ten years. You can find all the information you need about applying for a passport, including the location of your nearest passport facility, at www.travel.state.gov.

PASSPORT CHECKLIST

Here's what you need to bring with you when you apply for a passport:

- ✔ Fee payment, which was $97 at the time of publication

- ✔ Completed application form (available online)

- ✔ Two identical passport-size photos

- ✔ A birth certificate or other proof of U.S. citizenship

- ✔ A valid photo ID

LOSE YOUR PASSPORT?

If you lose your passport in Madrid, head directly to the U.S. Embassy weekdays from 3:00 P.M. to 5:00 P.M. for assistance. If your passport expires when you're abroad, you can also renew it through the U.S. Embassy. For more information on handling lost passports and other emergencies, see Chapter 18, "Emergencies."

....

U.S. Embassy in Madrid Ⓐ C/ Serrano 75, Ⓣ 91 587 22 40, Ⓦ http://madrid.usembassy.gov, Ⓜ Núñez de Balboa

---

STUDENT VISAS

You must apply for a visa in person at your local Spanish consulate, which, depending on where you live, could be quite a haul to get to. To ensure that you don't make a long trip in vain, be as thorough as possible in putting together your application beforehand. Check your regional consulate's website for information on what documents you'll need to bring with you, as requirements may vary. Applications can take up to six weeks to process. While you're waiting, feel free to inundate the consulate with phone calls and emails—it may help hurry things along. You can find the location of your regional consulate on the website of the Embassy of Spain in the United States, www.spainemb.org.

STUDENT VISA CHECKLIST

Though it is imperative to check your regional consulate's website to know exactly what you need, the following are likely necessities:

- ✔ Three filled-out copies of the downloadable application forms

- ✔ A valid passport

- ✔ Three passport-size photos

- ✔ Information on your program (including an acceptance letter)

- ✔ Proof that you'll have financial support of at least $1,000 per month (such as a bank statement or a letter from your university stating that tuition has been paid)

- ✔ Proof of health insurance

- ✔ An application fee of $100, payable by money order

REGISTERING WITH THE U.S. EMBASSY

It's always a good idea to register your trip with the U.S. Embassy in Madrid at https://travel registration.state.gov/ibrs (choose the "long-term traveler" option if you'll be abroad for longer than six months). By providing information about your stay and your emergency contacts, you'll help the embassy find you quickly in the case of an emergency back home (or abroad). The embassy can also offer assistance if you're involved in an accident or are the victim of a crime—see Chapter 18, "Emergencies," for more information.

OTHER TYPES OF VISAS

If you hope to extend your stay after classes end or you have a nonstudent significant other who will be joining you during your time abroad, there are a few other types of visas you should know about:

- **Work visa:** A work visa is required for any nonstudent who intends to work in Spain. Work visas are notoriously difficult to get and require that you first find a Spanish employer willing to sponsor you. For more information on work visas, see Chapter 11, "Working."

- **Spouse visa:** A spouse visa is required if you are a nonstudent who plans to join your spouse while he or she is studying or working abroad. To apply, you must submit an application form—along with your spouse's application form and copies of your marriage certificate—to your nearest Spanish consulate. A spouse visa does not give you the right to work in Spain; however, if you find a job once you're there, having a spouse visa may help facilitate the process of getting a work visa.

- **Tourist visa:** Tourists who are just visiting Madrid don't need to worry about visas. The stamp you get in your passport is considered a tourist visa and permits you to visit countries in the Schengen area, an open-border zone whose participating countries include Austria, Belgium, Denmark, Finland, France, Germany, Greece, Iceland, Italy, Luxembourg, the Netherlands, Norway, Portugal, and Sweden. You're free to visit for up to ninety days over a six-month period, which begins on the day your passport is stamped when you enter Europe. The ninety days do not have to be consecutive, so days you spend outside the Schengen area—for example, if you take a trip to London or Krakow—don't count against your total. After ninety days, your tourist visa expires and can be renewed only after the six-month period is up.

> ### KEEPING IT LEGAL
>
> If you enter Spain on a tourist visa and stay longer than ninety days over a six-month period, guess what? You're considered an illegal alien. When you attempt to leave or reenter Spain, or should you have a run-in with police, you may be detained, deported, or forced to pay hefty fines.

STUDY-ABROAD CHECKLIST

Before packing your bags and heading to the airport with a big ole excited grin on your face, make sure you've checked the following off your list:

- Get a **passport.**

- Get a **student visa.**

- Book your **plane ticket.**

- Arrange **housing** if it's not already provided for you (or a hotel/hostel if you plan to do an apartment search once you've arrived in Madrid). See Chapter 4, "Finding Housing."

- Apply for an International Student Identity Card (**ISIC**), which can get you great discounts on travel, entertainment, and more.

- Set up **online financial statements** and bill payment.

- ✓ Arrange **absentee voting** if you'll be abroad during an election.

- ✓ Schedule a predeparture **physical** if you need one. You don't need to get any particular vaccinations before going to Spain, as long as your routine vaccinations, such as tetanus-diphtheria and measles, are up to date.

- ✓ Get a copy of your **medical records,** especially if you have a preexisting condition for which you'll need treatment abroad.

- ✓ Make sure you have adequate **health insurance** coverage (your university should help with this). See Chapter 9, "Health," for more information on health insurance options and getting medical treatment while in Madrid.

- ✓ Set up **VoIP service** with your friends and family so that you can keep in touch for free. See Chapter 8, "Staying in Touch."

- ✓ Refill any **prescription drugs** you need. See Chapter 9, "Health," for your options when it comes to buying prescription medications in Madrid.

- ✓ Stock up on **over-the-counter drugs** such as aspirin and cold medicine. Your American drugs will come in handy down the line when you need to restock your medicine cabinet—showing the Spanish pharmacist your American product may help him or her find you the Spanish equivalent.

- ✓ Make a photocopy of your passport and leave it, along with your Madrid **contact info,** with your family.

✔ Call your **credit card** companies to inform them you'll be abroad so that you don't receive concerned phone calls about fraudulent overseas transactions.

✔ Stock up on **American products** you may not be able to get abroad, such as your favorite brands of deodorant, hair products, moisturizer, or allergy medicine.

✔ Stock up on **clothes** and other essentials. (You'll find prices to be much higher than in the United States—especially because you'll be paying in euros, and sales happen just two times a year!)

✔ Enough already. Now **get going!**

10 SONGS TO DOWNLOAD FOR YOUR FLIGHT TO MADRID

1. "La Puerta de Alcalá," Ana Belén
2. "Quién me Iba a Decir," David Bisbal
3. "Spain," Chick Corea
4. "Holiday in Spain" Counting Crows
5. "Te Dejo Madrid," Shakira
6. "Daniel," Elton John
7. "Moralito" ("La Gota Fría"), Julio Iglesias
8. "Hoy No me Puedo Levantar," Mecano
9. "Boots of Spanish Leather," Bob Dylan
10. "Lo Echamos a Suertes," Ella Baila Sola

2. The Neighborhoods

Ask ten Madrileños to name their favorite neighborhoods, and you'll get ten unique responses. What's more, their descriptions of where those neighborhoods start and end will also vary. Most young city-dwellers refer to each *zona,* or area of the city, by the nearest metro station. Many older locals provide only street names when describing the location of a store, school, or restaurant. That isn't to say, however, that foreigners get lost easily in Madrid. The downtown area is manageable on foot, with the overwhelming majority of tourist sights, such as the Plaza Mayor, Prado Museum, and Royal Palace, within walking distance of one another.

La Puerta del Sol is the city's tourist center, and most students and foreigners choose to live within walking distance or a short metro trip of Sol. Many neighborhoods, mostly residential, aren't mentioned in this chapter for the simple fact that their distance from Madrid's center renders them unlikely destinations for students and young people. However, if you choose to go exploring, you'll find plenty to recommend—including tightly knit neighborhood communities and bars where you're guaranteed to be the only non-Madrileño!

ARGÜELLES/MONCLOA
Ⓜ **Ciudad Universitaria, Argüelles, Moncloa, Islas Filipinas**

This large chunk of northwestern Madrid surrounds the Ciudad Universitaria metro stop and is therefore home to many students. Largely residential, Argüelles and Moncloa provide a calmer atmosphere than you'll find in other neighborhoods. However, they're so close to Madrid's public universities that you're bound to find pockets of students searching for the few neighborhood nightclubs aimed at young people.

WHAT YOU'LL SEE:

- Groups of students taking a break from Madrid's largest university, **Complutense,** which is right in the middle of the neighborhood. Ⓜ Cuidad Universitaria

- Cheap, student-filled bars and cafes

- **Parque del Oeste,** the other big park in Madrid after Retiro and a popular playground for young children. Ⓜ Moncloa

- The **Teleférico,** a cable railway that goes from the Parque del Oeste to Casa de Campo and offers amazing views of the Palacio Real and the Basílica de San Francisco el Grande. Ⓜ Argüelles

- **Museo de América,** which houses artifacts and objects from Latin America procured during Spain's colonial days. Ⓐ Avenida de los Reyes Católicos 6, Ⓣ 91 549 26 41, Ⓜ Moncloa

- **Arco de la Victoria,** commissioned by Franco in 1956 as a tribute to the Nationalist Army. Ⓜ Moncloa

AUSTRIAS/OPERA
Ⓜ **Opera, Tirso de Molina**

You'll find two of the city's most majestic plazas here. The expansive Plaza Mayor, a brief walk from Sol, is a central meeting point whose traditional restaurants provide *terrazas* (outdoor seating) that are perfect for taking in the square's beauty. The Plaza del Oriente is bordered by the grand Palacio Real, Teatro Real opera house, and Catedral de la Almudena, a Catholic cathedral notable for its odd mix of old-style and modernist designs. Apartment rentals here are justifiably expensive and likely to be out of student range, but the beauty of this neighborhood is best appreciated by those simply passing through.

WHAT YOU'LL SEE:

- **Palacio Real,** which is still used by the Spanish royal family for state events. Ⓐ C/ de Bailén, Ⓣ 91 454 88 00, Ⓜ Opera

- **Plaza Mayor,** the throbbing heart of the city. Ⓜ Sol

- **Mercado de San Miguel,** Madrid's only market constructed out of iron. Ⓐ near the Plaza Mayor, Ⓜ Sol

- **Plaza del Oriente,** Madrid's largest square. Ⓜ Opera

- **Monasterio de las Descalzas Reales,** a functioning convent and museum. Its name, which means "the monastery of the barefoot royals," refers to the wealthy nuns who originally lived there. Ⓐ Plaza de las Descalzas, Ⓣ 91 542 00 59, Ⓜ Opera

- **Teatro Real,** Madrid's premier theater and opera house. Ⓐ Plaza Isabel II, S/N, Ⓣ 91 506 16 00, Ⓦ www.teatro-real. com, Ⓜ Opera

AZCA
Ⓜ Plaza Castilla, Santiago Bernabeu

Azca features Santiago Bernabeu Stadium, home of Madrid's beloved soccer team Real Madrid, and the intentionally leaning Torres Quio (also known as the Puerta de Europa, or "Gate to Europe"), as well as most of the city's skyscrapers. Big business occupies most of the rental space in this region, and outside of the busy Avenida de Brasil, night life is minimal.

WHAT YOU'LL SEE:

- **Torre Picasso,** one of Madrid's tallest office buildings

- **Santiago Bernabeu Stadium,** where Real Madrid plays. Ⓐ C/ Concha Espina 1, Ⓣ 91 398 43 00 or 90 232 43 24, Ⓦ www.realmadrid.com, Ⓜ Santiago Bernabeu

- **Avenida de Brasil,** a street with an abundance of nightclubs. It's a playground for Madrid's elite society.

- **Puerta de Europa,** two towers that are the world's first leaning high-rise buildings

CHAMBERÍ
Ⓜ Quevedo, Iglesia, Alonso Cano, Canal

Unlike Argüelles, this residential neighborhood is filled with families, not students. Areas of Chamberí, such as Quevedo and Iglesia, are within a twenty-minute walk of Sol but offer their inhabitants calm, quiet, and conveniences such as supermarkets and dry cleaners within minutes of home. In Chamberí, you'll see lots of locals going about their lives—and almost *no* tourists.

CHUECA
Ⓜ Chueca, Gran Vía

Housing the city's trendiest new restaurants and clothing boutiques, Chueca is best-known for being Madrid's gay neighborhood, and most of the establishments are gay-friendly. Chueca was once a dangerous neighborhood but has been revamped in recent years, and all young people will appreciate the hip, new spots and nouvelle cuisine that Chueca has to offer, including those options surrounding the always bustling Plaza de Chueca.

WHAT YOU'LL SEE:

- **Plaza de Chueca,** flanked on all sides by bars, restaurants, and clubs. Ⓜ Chueca
- **Calle de la Libertad,** a street that's brimming with excellent restaurants and cafes. Ⓜ Chueca
- **Gay Day,** Madrid's annual gay pride festival at the end of June

LA LATINA
Ⓜ**La Latina**

Madrid's trendiest locality fills up every Sunday with the young and beautiful. Tapas bars on Cava Baja and Cava Alta are known for modern twists to traditional Spanish dishes. While amenities such as supermarkets are scant for this area's residents, its bars are popular destinations for hip twenty- and thirty-somethings looking for fun.

WHAT YOU'LL SEE:

- **El Rastro,** Spain's most famous flea market. Ⓐbetween La Latina and Lavapiés

- **Plaza de la Paja,** or the "straw square," where farmers in medieval Madrid used to auction off their straw crops. ⓂLa Latina

- **Bar Cock,** a trendy bar popular with Spain's rich and famous that's named for its delicious but pricey cocktails. ⒶC/ Reina 16, Ⓣ91 532 28 26, ⓂGran Vía

- **La Puerta de Toledo,** a triumphal arch that once marked the southern limits of the old medieval town and the start of the old road to Toledo. ⓂPuerto de Toledo

- **Basílica de San Francisco el Grande,** which has one of the largest domes in the world, measuring 108 feet across. ⒶPlaza de San Francisco, Ⓣ 91 365 38 00, ⓂLa Latina

- **La Cebada,** one of Spain's oldest authentic markets. ⒶPlaza de La Cebada 15, ⓂLa Latina

LAVAPIÉS
Ⓜ**Lavapiés, Embajadores**

Recent immigrants from Arab and Asian countries have turned Lavapiés into a melting pot of cultures (and the closest thing Madrid has to a Chinatown). Just one metro stop south of Sol, this neighborhood is where you can go to find cheap ingredients for cooking Indian or Moroccan cuisine.

WHAT YOU'LL SEE:

- **Plaza Tirso de Molina,** named for Spain's famous Golden Age playwright. ⓜ Tirso de Molina

- The **Corrala,** the only remaining building of the working-class apartment complexes that characterized the neighborhood's architecture during the sixteenth century. ⓐ corner of C/ Mesón de Paredes and C/ Tributete, ⓜ Lavapiés

- **Filmoteca Cine Doré,** the cheapest theater in Madrid, showing classic and independent films. There are outdoor screenings in the summer. ⓐ C/ Santa Isabel 3, ⓣ 91 549 00 11, ⓜ Antón Martín

MALASAÑA
ⓜ Tribunal, Noviciado, Bilbao

Like its neighbor Chueca, Malasaña is a formerly dangerous area, once known for the drunks and junkies who congregated in the Plaza de Dos de Mayo. The neighborhood has since been cleaned up and transformed into a center of alternative culture. Its rebirth has been fueled by teenagers and twenty-somethings who cram themselves into the bohemian bars, cafes, and restaurants of Malasaña's narrow streets.

WHAT YOU'LL SEE:

- Groups of *gamberros,* Spain's alternative teenagers or punks, who usually congregate in the **Plaza de Dos de Mayo**. ⓜ Tribuna

- **La Ida,** a small bar famous for its cañas, where all the cool kids meet up. ⓐ C/ Colón 7, ⓣ 91 522 91 07, ⓜ Tribunal

- **Templo de Debod,** an Egyptian temple that was moved to Madrid in 1968, block by block, from its original location along the Nile River. ⓐ Paseo del Pintor Rosales, ⓣ 91 366 74 15, ⓜ Ventura Rodríguez

- **El 2De,** one of the neighborhood's most popular local bars. ⓐ in the Plaza de Dos de Mayo, behind the Iglesia de las Maravillas, ⓜ Tribunal

SALAMANCA/RETIRO

Ⓜ **Serrano, Velazquez, Goya, Ibiza, Lista, Nuñez de Balboa, Banco de España**

The wealthiest, cleanest part of the city center is home to the *gente pija,* which means either preppy or snobby people, depending on intonation and context. Its wide streets, occasional bike lanes, and proximity to the Parque del Buen Retiro make walking convenient. The Paseo del Prado, just outside the park, is where you'll find the Prado and the Museo Thyssen-Bornemisza, which, along with the Reina Sofía, form a triad of must-see museums. Those with expensive tastes will enjoy the high-end shopping on Calle Goya and Calle Serrano.

WHAT YOU'LL SEE:

- **The Prado,** the must-see destination of any self-respecting visitor to Madrid. Ⓐ Paseo del Prado, S/N, Ⓣ 91 330 28 00, Ⓦ www.museoprado.es, Ⓜ Atocha, Banco de España

- **Museo Thyssen-Bornemisza,** featuring mostly European art. Ⓐ Paseo del Prado 8, Ⓣ 91 369 01 51, Ⓦ www.museothyssen.org, Ⓜ Atocha, Banco de España

- **La Puerta de Alcala,** the official entranceway into the city . Ⓜ Retiro

- **Parque del Buen Retiro,** Madrid's version of New York's Central Park. It's a true urban oasis, complete with wide-open green spaces, winding walking paths, and a pond where you can rent a rowboat and romance your sweetheart (or watch the romancing in action). Ⓜ Retiro

- **La Bolsa,** Madrid's stock exchange building, located at the beginning of Paseo de Recoletos

- **Calle de Goya and Calle de Serrano,** Madrid's premier high-end shopping streets. Ⓜ Goya, Serano

- **Plaza de Colón,** which was erected in honor of Christopher Colombus and has a large wall-like monument celebrating Spain's discovery of America. Ⓜ Colón

SOL/HUERTAS
Ⓜ Sol, Sevilla, Antón Martín

La Puerta del Sol is a large plaza that is Madrid's center in every sense of the word. If you don't like crowds, noise, and tourists, you'd best stay away from Sol, but it won't be easy. The multitude of traditional Spanish bars, Irish pubs, shops, and famous pedestrian-only streets, such as Preciados and Huertas, will be a frequent destination of all your friends.

WHAT YOU'LL SEE:

- **Centro de Arte Reina Sofía,** home to Picasso's *Guernica.* Ⓐ C/ Santa Isabel 52, Ⓣ 91 467 50 62, Ⓦ www.museoreina sofia.es, Ⓜ Atocha

- The famous **bronze bear statue** (and tourists waiting to take their picture with it) on the corner of Calle del Carmen, one of Sol's busiest shopping streets. Ⓜ Sol

- The larger-than-life **Tío Pepe sign,** which works like the North Star for tourists who get lost. Ⓜ Sol

- The **Carlos III horse statue,** a popular meeting spot for groups exiting at the Sol metro stop and a reminder of Spain's glory days as one of Europe's most powerful countries during the eighteenth century. Ⓜ Sol

- **La Mallorquina,** one of Madrid's oldest and finest bakeries. Ⓐ Puerta del Sol 8, Ⓣ 91 521 12 01, Ⓜ Sol

- **Calle de la Montera,** a notorious red-light district, with prostitutes lining both sides of the street at all hours. Ⓜ Sol

- **Chocolatería San Ginés,** one of Madrid's best places to get *churros y chocolate* (long, thin doughnuts and hot chocolate). Ⓐ C/ Arenal 11, Ⓣ 91 365 65 46, Ⓜ Sol

- **Puerta del Sol**—the very center of Spain, indicated by a plaque near the Casa de Correos. Ⓜ Sol

- **Botín,** which was established in 1725 and is, according to the *Guinness Book of World Records,* the world's oldest restaurant. Ⓐ Cuchilleros 17, Ⓣ 91 366 42 17, Ⓜ Sol

SPANISH ADDRESSES

When deciphering Spanish addresses, keep these clues in mind:

- C/ means *Calle* (street).
- Avda means *Avenida* (avenue).
- S/N means there's no street number.
- Numerals with ° after them indicate the floor number.

5 PLACES WHERE YOU'LL FIND AMERICAN STUDENTS

1. **O'Conell Street:** This Irish pub in Sol sells a bucket of six beers for €14—talk about stretching your *centimos* (pennies). ⒶC/ Espoz y Mina 7, Ⓣated91 531 64 19, ⓂSol, Sevilla

2. **Shooters:** Grab your friends and hit this pool hall for the night. Think you've got game? It also hosts tournaments for serious players. ⒶC/ Gran Vía 31, Ⓣ91 522 40 10, ⓂGran Vía

3. **Triskel Tavern:** This rustic pub in Malasaña has Celtic-influenced interior decorating, but its biggest draw for students is its big selection of imported beers and Irish and Scottish whiskies. ⒶC/ San Vicente Ferrer 3, Ⓣ91 523 27 83, ⓂTribunal

4. **Palacio Gaviria:** This beautiful, circle-shaped club in Sol really does look like a palace on the inside, and the crowd is always international—and mostly American. ⒶC/ Arenal 9, Ⓣ91 526 60 69, ⓂSol

5. **The Chesterfield Club:** A quintessential Irish pub and American student hangout, Chesterfield serves barbequed ribs and cheap draft beer. Every Wednesday night, the bar turns into a club to host an international student party. Ⓐ C/ Serrano Jover 5, Ⓣ91 542 28 17, ⓂArgüelles

3. Getting Around

Madrid's public transportation system is user friendly and dependable. There are eleven subway lines, each of which is numbered and color coded to avoid confusion. If you're traveling outside of the city center, the city's buses are a good bet—although traffic renders them less useful in the more central areas. And if you're partying into the wee hours, head to the Plaza de Cibeles (Ⓜ Banco de España) and catch a *buho* (night bus), which departs every half hour, all night long.

Despite its 5 million inhabitants, Madrid's center is manageable for pedestrians. Weather permitting, walking is a great way to get around and to familiarize yourself with the city's sights and sounds. Unfortunately the center is not as friendly to cyclists, as there are no special bike lanes.

THE METRO

Madrid's metro provides efficient service—expect trains to arrive every two to five minutes on most lines during the day. The system has no express trains, which means some cars may arrive so overcrowded that you'll have to let one or more go before you can squeeze on. When planning a late night out, be aware that the metro system shuts down at around 1:30 A.M. and starts up again at around 6:00 A.M. Digital clocks have been installed on most platforms to let you know how much time will pass before the next train arrives.

Maps are free and available in most metro stations; simply ask the station attendant. Also, each station has a local street map posted by the station entrances and on the platforms. Check them out before heading up to street level in a neighborhood you don't know. For up-to-date maps and fare information, visit www.metromadrid.es, the official government website of Metro de Madrid, Madrid's metro system.

NAVIGATING THE SYSTEM

Every metro line runs in two directions, and with the exception of gray-colored line 6, which is circular, each has two ends. To make sure you're headed in the right direction, check the signs posted throughout the stations and on the platforms. To figure out how to get where you're going on the metro, ask yourself three questions:

1. *Where am I going?* Identify the station nearest your destination.

2. *Which line(s) will take me there?* If your starting and ending stations aren't on the same line, change trains where their lines meet on the metro map.

3. *In which direction am I traveling?* Follow station signs for your desired line and direction. Your direction is the end-station you're heading toward on the metro map. For example, if you want to take line 5, you'll go toward either Casa de Campo or Canillejas.

BUYING TICKETS

All metro tickets can be purchased inside any metro station from vending machines, which accept both cash and credit cards and provide English-language instructions, or from station attendants, who take only cash. You can buy a *sencillo* (single-ride ticket) or a ticket that holds several rides, such as the *metrobus,* which holds ten rides. Once inside the station, you'll use just one ride per trip, no matter how far in the system you travel or how many times you switch trains. After you dip your ticket at the turnstile, be sure to retrieve and keep your ticket for the rest of your trip—if a metro employee checks for tickets on the train, you could be fined if you don't have a ticket with you. Ten-ride tickets, unlimited-ride passes, and monthly passes can be used interchangeably on the metro and on buses.

MONTHLY PASSES

Unlike the single- and ten-trip tickets, monthly metro passes require an *abono* (identification card). Abonos cost approximately €1.20 and are available at any *tabacos* (smoke shops)—but not at metro stations. To buy one, you'll need to know your address and passport ID number (or Spanish resident or nonresident ID card number, if you have one) and bring a passport-size photograph. The abono must accompany the monthly pass, and no one is allowed to use the pass but you. The actual monthly pass can be purchased from vending machines or station attendants at metro stations. Each month you will need to purchase a new pass, but you don't have to get a new ID card. Always carry your monthly pass in the plastic sleeve it came with, along with your ID card, or it may be confiscated.

FARES

Fare prices depend on the *zona* in which you plan to travel. Zona A covers all of central Madrid, in which the overwhelming majority of foreign students and young people choose to live, work, and play; you'll likely go outside of it only rarely. Zona B1 extends into the outskirts of Madrid, and Zona B2 extends even farther. Other zones exist as well, but these are far outside the city. Here are some ticket options:

Single-ride ticket (*sencillo*): You'll pay €1 for travel within Zona A or €1.50 for travel within any zone.

Ten-ride ticket (*metrobus*): Ten-ride tickets will cost €6.15 for travel within Zona A.

Unlimited-ride tourist passes (*abono turístico*): These passes provide unlimited travel for short durations. You'll pay €3.80 for one day, €6.80 for two days, €9.00 for three days, €14.20 for five days, and €19.80 for seven days.

Monthly passes (*abono transporte*): A monthly pass is only cost-effective if you average two or more rides daily, so if you live in the center of the city or do a lot of walking, you probably won't need one. Passes will cost €39 for travel within Zona A, €45.25 for travel within Zona B1, and €51.65 for travel within Zona B2.

STUDENT DISCOUNTS

As a student, you can get special youth rates on monthly metro passes up until June of the year of your twenty-first birthday. With a youth discount, expect to pay €25.40 for travel within Zona A, €28.75 for travel within Zona B1, and €32.65 for travel within Zona B2.

BUSES

Traveling by bus in Madrid can be more confusing than traveling by metro, given that the city's bus network has more than 200 unique lines versus the metro's eleven lines. Bus travel, however, *can* be convenient, especially if you don't live close to a metro stop. Although the metro is almost always the faster option, special bus/taxi lanes have been instituted on many streets to bypass traffic, making service that much speedier. Still, be aware of the rush hours, which last approximately from 8:00 A.M. to 10:00 A.M., 2:00 P.M. to 4:00 P.M., and 7:00 P.M. to 9:00 P.M., because the increase in traffic will almost certainly add time to your trip. These are your bus options:

- **Regular buses:** Red buses and blue/white buses travel within Zona A. Green buses reach Madrid's suburbs and beyond (Zonas B1 and B2). Many of these buses begin their routes at one of a few main outdoor hubs, such as Plaza de Castilla in the north, Legazpi in the south, Avenida de América in the east, and Moncloa in the west.

- **Night buses:** Madrid's buhos run through the early morning on weekends. Additionally, there are twenty-four unique bus lines that leave, seven days a week, from the Plaza de Cibeles every half hour between 11:30 P.M. and 6:00 A.M. And new buhometros have recently begun. To catch one, go to the nearest metro stop and wait; they pass by every fifteen minutes from 1:00 A.M. to 5:45 A.M. on Friday and Saturday nights and on nights preceding holidays. The price is the same as a regular bus or metro ride, and you can use your regular ticket or pass.

NAVIGATING THE SYSTEM

At each bus stop, posters list the general direction of each bus, but they don't list every stop—there are simply too many. Each bus stop is serviced by a few distinct lines, so make sure you're boarding the right bus—Madrid's buses are identified by electronic panels on the front displaying the bus's line number and direction. Also make sure you're waiting on the appropriate side of the street, as each bus line runs in two directions. Arrows on the posted bus routes at each stop will indicate the direction of the line. Depending on the time of day, expect to wait anywhere between five and twenty minutes. Schedules are usually posted at the stops, but they're usually not accurate predictors of when your bus will actually arrive.

BUYING TICKETS

Ten-ride tickets, unlimited-ride passes, and monthly passes can be used interchangeably on the metro and bus systems. Single-ride tickets can be purchased directly from bus drivers. If you're using a ten-trip ticket, validate it by dipping it into the small machine near the front of the bus. Be sure to retrieve your ticket and hold onto it for the duration of your trip: If a bus employee boards the bus to check for tickets, you could be fined if you haven't validated yours or don't have it with you. To exit a bus, press one of the red buttons located on the support rods throughout the bus to get the next stop and leave through the back doors.

STAYING SAFE

In general, traveling by public transportation is perfectly safe in Madrid. Metro stations are mostly well lit and protected by security guards, making them safe no matter the hour. If you do have a problem, however, it will probably be pickpocketing (mugging occurs rarely). Try to board cars that are moderately full of passengers and keep your valuables close to you at all times.

TAXIS

Taxis in Madrid are moderately priced, reliable, and readily available anywhere in the city—but due to the relatively low cost of public transportation, Madrileños rarely use them. Late at night after the metro shuts down, however, competition for taxis can be quite fierce, and you may have to resort to looking for the nearest night bus. Although unauthorized cabs aren't common, make sure you're getting into an authorized metered cab, which will be white with a diagonal red stripe. If you live in the city's outskirts or need a 4:00 A.M. ride to the airport, call Radio Telefono Taxi, Madrid's largest private taxi company (91 547 82 00, www.radiotelefono-taxi.com) to arrange for a pick up.

TAXI FARES

The base taxi fare is €1.75 during the day, with supplemental charges at night or outside city limits. If you catch a taxi outside a bus or train station, there will be a €2.40 supplement, and rides from the airport carry an additional charge of €4.50. Each kilometer is €0.82 during the day and €0.95 at night; for a ten-minute ride, expect to pay around €5 or €6. Most cabs accept cash and credit cards, but be sure to ask your driver whether credit cards are accepted before getting in. Tipping isn't expected in taxis, especially for short trips, and most young Madrileños just pay the price on the meter. However, tips are certainly appreciated: Round the fare up to the nearest euro, or offer an extra euro or two if you're feeling generous.

BIKES

Between the constant, hectic automobile traffic and the lack of designated lanes, few Madrileños ride bicycles around the city. One exception is the scene every weekend at El Parque del Buen Retiro, Madrid's largest park, which fills with cyclists and rollerbladers. If you live too far away to bike there, you're allowed to carry bikes with you on the metro—but only on weekends and holidays.

New bikes range in price from €100 to €1,000, depending on the brand and style. If you're interested in buying a bike, El Corte Inglés (www.elcorteingles.es), Spain's only mega-department store, or the sporting goods chain Decathlon (www.decathlon.es) are both good places to start. For secondhand bikes, check out the weekly periodical *Segunda Mano* (www.segundamano.es), available at any newsstand, as well as Loquo (madrid.loquo.com) and Craigslist (http://madrid.craigslist.org).

RENTING A BIKE

Madrid has numerous bike rental shops. Day rentals for bikes are in the €10 to €15 range; bikes can also be rented by the weekend or week. Here are a few centrally located bike shops to check out:

Bike Spain Ⓐ C/ Carmen 17, Ⓣ 91 522 38 99, Ⓦ www.bikespain.info, Ⓜ Sol

By Bike Ⓐ Avda. de Menendez Pelayo 35, Ⓣ 90 287 64 83, Ⓜ Retiro, Ibiza

Ciclos Otero Ⓐ C/ Segovia 18–20, Ⓣ 91 547 32 25, Ⓦ www.oterociclos.es, Ⓜ La Latina, Tirso de Molina

GENERAL RULES OF THE ROAD FOR CYCLISTS

Cycling in Madrid can be treacherous. Keep these key points in mind:

- **Safety:** Although it's not legally required, you should always wear a helmet. And be vigilant when passing parked cars, as people often open their doors without looking first.

- **Equipment:** Your bike should be equipped with a headlight and a red taillight.

- **Traffic lights and signals:** You must obey all traffic lights and signals. Indicate that you intend to make a turn by using proper hand signals. Do not ride faster than any cars.

CARS

Driving in Madrid is not for the traffic-shy. Madrid is plagued by terrible traffic, and there's no avoiding the accidents, unsafe drivers, double-parked cars, and pollution caused by the driving multitudes. Measures such as highway carpool lanes that converge in Madrid have done little to alleviate the city's traffic problems. And dealing with traffic is just part of the problem—wait until you try parking! Motorbikes and scooters also remain a popular—if perilous—way to zip through the city's streets.

You'll probably have to do very little driving while you're in Madrid. If you're set on exploring Spain or Europe from behind the wheel, see Chapter 17, "Going Away," for information on renting a car.

GENERAL RULES OF THE ROAD FOR DRIVERS

For the most part, the same road rules you'd follow in the United States are also applicable in Madrid. Here are a few reminders:

- **Passing:** The left lane is for passing and *only* passing; linger there too long, and you'll learn some unsavory new Spanish words.

- **Double parking:** On smaller, less busy streets, cars are frequently double-parked. If you find yourself blocked in, the correct protocol is nonstop honking combined with dirty looks for as long as it takes to get that other driver to move.

- **Speed limits:** In Spain, the speed limit on highways is 120 kilometers per hour (kph) or approximately 75 miles per hour (mph); within towns, expect the speed limit to be 50 kph or 30 mph.

TRAINS

The Spanish train system, which is run by the national rail operator Renfe, will take you almost anywhere you want to go in the country. In addition to trains reaching other cities in Spain and Europe, a network of commuter trains called *Cercanías* extend throughout the greater Madrid area. Cercanías are faster and more comfortable than the metro, but stations with Cercanías service are few and far between in central Madrid (metro maps indicate service with a small red *C*).

Prices depend on the distance of your trip, and multi-trip vouchers are available—these can be purchased from vendors and easy-to-use machines in any Cercanías station. Single-trip prices range from €1 to €4. If you have a monthly metro/bus pass, you can use it on Cercanías, making any travel between stations in Zona A essentially free. If you begin in Zona A and finish your route outside the city center, however, you'll have to buy a ticket. Hang on to your train ticket: Unlike the metro, train tickets are required to exit stations. For information about destinations, schedules, and fares visit www.renfe.es, Renfe's detailed website.

LONG-DISTANCE TRAINS

Longer-distance trains leave from one of two stations. Atocha handles the overwhelming majority of long-distance trains entering and exiting Madrid. But other trains leave from and arrive at Chamartín Station, a smaller station located in the north of the city. Both stations are accessible by metro and bus. For more information on long-distance travel inside and outside of Spain, see "The Spanish Rail System" in Chapter 17.

TO AND FROM THE AIRPORT

Madrid is served by Barajas. Transportation to and from the airport was simpler before 2006, when Barajas opened its fourth terminal, T4. To move from the main airport building to the new T4 hub, you can take a free shuttle bus that runs every three minutes. Here are your options for traveling to and from the airport:

- **Metro:** If you're leaving from central or northeastern Madrid and aren't carrying too much luggage, the metro is the easiest way to get to the airport. The pink line 8 takes off at Nuevos Ministerios and reaches the airport at the stop Aeropuerto. Be aware that you'll either have to walk ten minutes through the airport to reach T2 departures or walk outside and find the shuttle to T4, depending on where you're going. It takes about forty minutes to get to the airport by metro, excluding the shuttle ride to T4, which adds an extra twenty to thirty minutes.

- **Bus:** City buses departing from the Avenida de América transport hub stop at the airport. Line 200 provides service to T1 and T2 Arrivals, while Line 204 goes to T4 Arrivals. It takes about fifteen minutes to get to the airport from the city center by bus, but be sure to leave time for unexpected traffic delays, which could add significant time to your trip.

- **Taxi:** A taxi is the easiest way to get into the city. Take rides only from registered taxis, which are usually lined up outside the arrivals area. Taxis to and from the airport should cost approximately €15 to €25; if the traffic isn't terrible, the ride should be about twenty minutes to or from the city center.

TRAVELERS WITH DISABILITIES

Madrid's hilly terrain and old, narrow streets make it challenging for those with disabilities. Few metro stations are equipped with elevators. Public facilities, including universities, healthcare centers, civic buildings, and libraries, are generally well-equipped with ramps and elevators, but don't expect the same accessibility at restaurants, bars, and other small establishments.

5 OTHER MUST-SEE CITIES IN SPAIN

1. **Barcelona:** Located along Spain's eastern coast, Barcelona has gorgeous beaches, stunning architecture by Gaudi, amazing restaurants, and arguably the best night life in the country.

2. **Cadiz**: Come to this beautiful city along the southern coast in February for El Carnaval, Spain's wildest festival, when people dress in costumes and parade through the city streets. Although it's now a purely secular—and fun—celebration, it was originally considered a way to indulge before Lenten fasting began.

3. **Cordoba:** Cordoba has a rich *mudejar* history (a combination of Arabic, Jewish, and Catholic cultures) and is home to the Mezquita, one of the most awe-inspiring architectural masterpieces in Spain.

4. **Granada:** Home of the Alhambra, an immense palace and mosque built in the thirteenth century, Granada is also famous for its large population of college students and free tapas that accompany the drinks at most bars.

5. **Seville:** Ultratraditional Seville has winding cobblestone streets and a stunning cathedral, not to mention a reputation as one of the best places to see an authentic flamenco performance.

4. Finding Housing

F inding accommodations in Madrid is not difficult—the overwhelming majority of foreigners find housing on their own within a week of their arrival. Word of mouth, the Internet, and bulletin boards in various cafes, bookstores, schools, and bars are the most common search resources.

Sharing an apartment with other young people is the most common housing arrangement. Many apartments come furnished, with a washing machine, refrigerator, microwave, sofa, and bed—some even include kitchen utensils and bed linens. If you prefer to start from scratch, plenty of unfurnished residences are available as well, at about the same cost.

APARTMENT LISTINGS

The cheapest way to find an apartment in Madrid is to do it without the help of a broker or third-party agent. Be quick in responding to ads, and don't shy away from being persistent or making early-morning phone calls. Online listings tend to be more up to date and useful; search print publications only when they are hot off the press.

Listings are divided into two categories: *pisos compartidos* (shared apartments) and *pisos de alquiler* (apartments for rent). If you're looking to meet new (possibly Spanish-speaking) people, not spend too much money, or stay only short-term, then shared apartments are your best bet. Because you're essentially subletting, you avoid the hassle of having to sign a lease, buy furniture, or put utilities in your name. Check out the websites for *Segunda Mano* (www.segundamano. es), Loquo (madrid.loquo.com), Idealista (www.idealista. com), and Craigslist (http://madrid.craigslist.org), each of which lists hundreds of new rentals every day.

APARTMENT HUNTING TIPS

Here are a few key things to keep in mind during you apartment search:

- The rental market is first-come, first-served, so don't be late to any appointments, and be prepared to decide quickly. Owners and tenants might request a *señal* (a sign of your interest), often in the form of a small deposit, immediately upon your visit.

- Remember that if it sounds too good to be true, it probably is. As in the United States, Spanish ad-writers don't hesitate to stretch the truth about an apartment's size, location, or brightness.

- Be aware that many landlords are reluctant to rent to students, especially foreign students. On the other hand, some apartment owners actually *prefer* to rent to students, sometimes even mentioning Erasmus, the Europewide university exchange program, in their ads.

- Bring a checklist with you when you visit prospective apartments. Be sure to check for things such as storage space, electrical outlets, water pressure, whether you can hear noise from the street or neighboring apartments, and whether appliances such as the refrigerator and stove work.

FINANCIAL ASSURANCES

Pisos de alquiler (apartments for rent) are usually advertised by individual owners and occasionally by real estate agencies. If you want your own place or to rent out a two- or three-bedroom apartment with friends, be prepared to present documentation proving your financial abilities. A *nómina* is a monthly pay statement from your employer, which demonstrates your salary and contract status. You can also provide an *aval,* which is collateral—six months or even a year of rent that your bank freezes in your account and makes payable to your landlord in the event that you fail to pay him or her.

Freezing this much money will prove difficult for anyone without a lot of spare cash handy. If faced with a request for aval, don't give up without a fight. Most owners are open to some degree of negotiation, so go ahead and bargain. Ask whether they'll accept a letter from your bank confirming your good credit, or offer a security deposit equal to more than one month's rent. If a parent can act as a guarantor, offer that option as well.

BROKERS

Enlisting the services of a broker can take a lot of the headache out of your apartment search. A broker will facilitate your search, negotiating directly between you and prospective landlords. Of course, the catch is that you'll have to pay a broker's fee, which usually equals a month's rent or 10 percent of a year's rent. One reputable agency is Tecnopiso (www.tecnopiso.es); however, there are countless agencies in the city.

If you choose to search on your own, be aware that some listings are posted by brokers who are hired by apartment owners. Although the ads won't specifically mention a broker's affiliation with a real estate agency, you might be able to figure it out if the broker's email address is for a business rather than an individual or from other information provided in the ad. This is important to know because, in some cases, you'll still be required to cover the broker's fee (in addition to a security deposit and the first month's rent).

APARTMENT-LISTING LEXICON

In Spain, building floors are numbered differently than in the United States. What Americans think of as the first, or ground, floor is called the *bajo*. Up one flight of stairs is the *principal* floor; up two flights of stairs is the first floor, called the *primer;* and so on. Here are some other common terms you'll find in apartment ads:

amplio	spacious
amueblado	furnished
ascensor	elevator
baño	full bathroom
calefacción	heat
cama de matrimonio	full-size bed
cama individual	twin bed
estudio	studio
gastos incluidos	expenses are included in the price
habitaciones or *dormitories*	bedrooms
lavadora	washing machine
lavavajillas	dishwasher
*sin amueblar	vacío*	unfurnished / empty

APARTMENT PRICES

Be prepared to pay up to three months' rent before moving in: the first month's rent, plus a security deposit equivalent to one or two months' rent. The security deposit will be refunded upon your departure, assuming you leave the place in decent condition. If you go through an agency, the broker's fee is added on top of this, bringing the total to four months' rent up front—and sometimes more.

With a few exceptions, sharing an apartment is your most cost-effective option. Sharing a two-bedroom with a roommate might cost only €400 a month. Sharing an apartment with three or more bedrooms can cost you as little as €200 a month. If you want to live alone, a studio near the city center will range from €450 to €650 a month. A one-bedroom in the same area will cost you €600 a month or much more.

LEASES

The first lease you sign in Madrid will likely be short-term, lasting only six months or a year. If your Spanish isn't quite up to reading legal documents, ask your future landlord for a copy of the contract beforehand, giving you time to go over it or pass it along to someone more competent in the language. At the very least, bring a Spanish speaker with you when signing, just to make sure that all terms and conditions are clear. If you're signing a lease with friends or strangers, you're all responsible for each other: If one person doesn't pay, it's everyone's problem.

UNDERSTANDING LEASES

Expect a standard lease to include the following:

- The amount of rent, when it's due, how it should be paid, and any utilities included

- Whether you can leave before the end of the lease and the procedure for giving notice, as well as rules about subletting

- The furnishings included (An inventory is usually conducted by a third party at the beginning and end of tenancy and is used to assess damages when the tenancy concludes.)

- Who is responsible for repairs

- The amount of the security deposit, which will be held either by the landlord or the company that manages the property (If the deposit will be placed in an interest-earning account, this should be specified in the lease.)

HOMESTAYS

A homestay is an arrangement in which you live with a Spanish household for a semester or school year, with your own bedroom, a bathroom that may or may not be shared, laundry service, and meals. Homestays may be with an actual family unit or may be limited to a grandmother-type *señora*.

The advantage of a homestay is that it basically forces you to immerse yourself in the language and culture, which is more difficult to do if you're living in a studio apartment or student residence. If you get along well with your host family, a homestay can be incredibly rewarding. However, if the family is rigid, disinterested, or invasive, the benefits of this option will most likely be overshadowed.

Before deciding whether a homestay is for you, be careful to assess your eating preferences. Meals can be hit or miss depending on your host's culinary skills (and your level of pickiness). Refusing meals may create friction in the household. And because board is included in the price of a homestay, you'll wind up paying double if you feel the need to eat out frequently. If you are a vegetarian or have any food allergies or dietary restrictions, you might need more control over meal preparation than homestays allow.

If you'd like to pursue a homestay, discuss this option with your school. If your program can't match you with a Spanish family, try combing apartment listings for homestay notices. Some Madrileños with bedrooms to rent advertise their openings on bulletin boards around Ciudad Universitaria and in *Segunda Mano* (www.segundamano.es). Rates for homestays vary depending on the specific accommodations that you or your school arrange.

5 MADRID
APARTMENT QUIRKS

1. **Teeny, tiny elevators:** Aside from being inhumanly small (we're talking two people max), some elevators have doors that you have to pull open manually. Try doing that with bags of groceries in your hands.

2. **Bidets:** Although uncommon in the United States, you'll find bidets in most bathrooms in Spain (and in other European countries).

3. **Automatic lights:** It's great that the Spanish want to conserve energy, but it's not so great when the automatic timer lights in the stairwells and halls turn off, leaving you in pitch blackness, groping along the wall for a switch. And if it's tough when you're sober, imagine what it's like after a few glasses of sangria.

4. **Insufficient power outlets:** With only one outlet in most rooms, you'll need to stock up on power strips and extension cords.

5. **No clothes dryers:** Any Madrileño will swear that drying your clothes on a line is better than using a dryer because clothes last longer and stay softer. But that means saying adiós to washing your favorite jeans an hour before going out—now you'll have to plan ahead.

5. Shopping

For American students raised with the convenience of 24-hour, one-stop shopping, food shopping in Madrid can be an exercise in frustration. Most grocery options are closed on Sundays, while others shut down at midday for the siesta, and in spring and summer most markets close before sundown. Some neighborhoods—such as Sol, Malasaña, and Chueca—have no supermarkets because of their narrow streets, which make it impossible for trucks to make deliveries; you may be able to find small *bodegas* (small corner shops) and municipal markets within walking distance, but specialty items may require a metro trip. However, Madrid is a major metropolis, and gourmet shops, American brands, Asian foods, and late-night shopping are all available somewhere in the city—you just have to do a little footwork.

And for nonfood-related shopping, Madrid will not disappoint—even if you're on the tightest of student budgets. You may be tempted to pop into a few cool boutiques as you make your way around town or browse in one of the city's luxury retailers, but to maximize your purchasing power, head straight to El Rastro, Madrid's famous flea market—a landmark in and of itself.

SUPERMARKETS

While Madrid's wide range of *supermercados* (supermarkets) vary in size, price, and quality, most carry almost any type of food you could want, just don't expect to see as large a selection of brands as you would in the United States. Most supermarkets are open from 9:00 A.M. to 9:00 P.M. Monday through Saturday.

In general, prices of individual items are comparable to those in the United States. Two major exceptions are cheese and yogurt, which are much cheaper in Spain. Día and Plus are the cheapest supermarket options in every sense of the word: Their prices are low, but they also charge for plastic bags. For a slightly more exciting shopping experience, head to the department store El Corte Inglés. Most locations feature a large supermarket with an ample selection (and high prices), and some also have a *tienda del gourmet* (gourmet or speciality shop) section, with harder-to-find international products and brand names.

- Caprabo ⓦ www.caprabo.es
- Champion ⓦ www.champion.es
- El Corte Inglés ⓦ www.elcorteingles.com
- Eroski ⓦ www.eroski.es
- Día ⓦ www.dia.es
- Mercadona ⓦ www.mercadona.es
- Plus ⓦ www.plus-supermercados.es

GROCERY SHOPPING 101

Keep these facts in mind when you're heading out to the grocery aisles:

- **Quantities are metric:** Most Spanish products are labeled according to the metric system. Take note of these conversions: 1kg = 2.2 lbs; 100 g = 3.5 oz; and 1L = 2.1 pints.

- **Milk isn't refrigerated:** While some markets offer a minor selection of refrigerated *leche fresca* (fresh milk), most milk is sold in a plastic carton called a Tetra-Pak, which can be stored at room temperature for months. Once opened, it must be refrigerated and lasts only as long as fresh milk does.

SPECIALTY FOODS

Living in Madrid, you'll often see your neighbors pushing *carritos* (small carts) around as they go grocery shopping at various small markets and specialty shops. Some of this is due to necessity—if there are no supermarkets nearby, for example—but more often it's by preference. The food at these local stores is fresh and of a high quality, the selection is great, and merchants are happy to offer advice on food selection or preparation.

BAKERIES

Fresh bread is so important at Spanish meals that *panadería* or *pastelería* (bakeries) often stay open on Sundays. Although supermarkets also offer fresh bread, bakeries manage to stay in business by offering pastries and desserts as well. You can choose from a wide variety of types of bread, so experiment until you find your favorite.

PRODUCE SHOPS

Some fruit and vegetable shops are self-service, which means you must take the items you want, bag them, and sometimes weigh them, using a key number that you'll input on the electronic scale. At other markets, you tell an employee what you want, and he or she retrieves the items for you. Because these small produce shops are usually family owned and operated, clerks can often provide excellent advice about the produce you're selecting.

BUTCHERS AND FISHMONGERS

Buying steak in a *carnicería* (butcher shop) follows the same protocol as picking up chicken in a *pollería* (poultry shop) or fresh fish in a *pescadería* (fish shop). Quantity is determined by weight in kilograms, although there are some exceptions. If you want beef or chicken breast in a filet, just ask the butcher. If you're overwhelmed by the selection, want advice on what meat or fish would be best for the dish you want to prepare, or need cooking instructions, ask the butcher or fishmonger for his thoughts.

INTERNATIONAL GROCERS

To meet the demands of a fast-growing immigrant population, Madrid has seen a number of shops offering exclusively foreign products open in recent years. For example, Chinese, Thai, and Japanese cuisines, once nonexistent in the city, are now in demand. A number of bodegas in neighborhoods with immigrant populations offer foreign fare. In addition, you can now find large Asian supermarkets, such as the Supermercado Oriental. Hespen & Suarez and Taste of America offer a variety of products from around the world, including American brands.

Supermercado Oriental Ⓐ outside the Príncipe Pío mall, Ⓜ Príncipe Pío

Hespen & Suarez Ⓐ C/ Barceló 15, Ⓣ 90 225 91 25, Ⓜ Tribunal; Ⓐ C/ Príncipe de Vergara 93, Ⓣ 91 564 28 77, Ⓜ Avenida de América

Taste of America Ⓐ C/ Serrano 149, Ⓣ 91 562 16 32, Ⓜ República Argentina

SPECIAL DIETS

Tofu-based products and other veggie lifesavers are hard to come by, so international grocers and large supermarkets in ethnic areas are your best bet. Check out Happy Cow (www.happycow.net), a website that tracks vegetarian-friendly restaurants and shops in Europe. To find kosher foods, try the neighborhoods surrounding the Comunidad Israelita de Madrid synagogue; for halal foods try the areas around the Islamic Cultural Center.

Comunidad Israelita de Madrid (kosher) Ⓐ C/ Balmes 3, Ⓣ 91 446 30 86, Ⓜ glesia

Carneceria Elias (kosher) Ⓐ C/ Viriato 35, Ⓣ 91 446 78 47, Ⓜ Iglesia

La Escudilla (kosher) Ⓐ C/ Santísima Trinidad 16, Ⓣ 91 445 73 80, Ⓜ Iglesia

Islamic Cultural Center (halal) Ⓐ Salvador de Madariaga 4, Ⓣ 91 326 26 10, Ⓜ Barrio de la Concepción

LATE NIGHT SHOPPING

Craving a midnight snack? OpenCor (www.opencor.es) is open from 8:00 A.M. to 2:00 A.M. 365 days a year. It has a little bit of everything: bread, produce, meat, snacks, books, newspapers, and more. Sprint (www.repsolypf.com) is a convenience store similar to 7-Eleven that stays open twenty-four hours a day.

FARMERS' MARKETS

If you want a dose of local culture, try one of Madrid's municipal markets. These mostly indoor markets have become somewhat less popular in recent years, thanks to the influx of supermarkets, but plenty still open on a daily basis. Each market maintains its own schedule;

however, most open around 9:00 A.M., shut down for lunch at 2:00 P.M., and then reopen from 5:00 P.M. to 8:00 P.M.

Farmers' markets can be found in most neighborhoods. Unlike in the United States, farmers' markets are typically located on the ground floors or basement levels of buildings. Prices are comparable to supermarkets'. Here are a few of the most popular markets in Madrid:

La Cebada This famous food market, which sells fish, meats, fruits, and vegetables, is one of Spain's oldest authentic markets. Visit La Cebada to complement your shopping at the nearby flea market El Rastro. Ⓐ Plaza de La Cebada 15, Ⓜ La Latina

La Paz This small but well-stocked market offers high-quality produce, an impressive array of cheeses from around the world, and other ingredients for discerning cooks. Ⓐ C/ Ayala 28, Ⓜ Velazquez

Maravillas If you want to experience the bustle of a large Spanish market, check out Maravillas—it's one of the largest in Madrid. You can also shop for flowers, jewelry, and other items. Most people consider the prices here to be cheaper than those at other markets. Ⓐ C/ Bravo Murillo 122, Ⓜ Cuatro Caminos

San Miguel Madrid's only market constructed out of iron, San Miguel was built in 1915 and still sells large quantities of the freshest and cheapest produce and baked goods. Unfortunately, the rise in supermarkets has forced several of the market's stalls to close down. Ⓐ Plaza de San Miguel, by the Plaza Mayor, Ⓜ Sol

ONE-STOP SHOPPING

Though one-stop shopping isn't as ubiquitous in Spain as it is in the United States, Madrid's outskirts have recently sprouted some huge all-in-one megastores—known as *hipermercados*—that offer everything from blue jeans and tomato sauce to laundry detergent and DVDs. While a few hipermercados can be reached by public transportation, most are accessible by car only. If you have a long shopping list, check out the following stores; see websites for store locations:

Alcampo There are eleven Alcampo locations in Madrid, including the Vaguada shopping center in the Barrio del Pilar neighborhood. Ⓦ www.alcampo.es

Carrefour Despite having seventeen stores in Madrid, no stores are located anywhere near the city center. If you make the trek, however, you'll find anything and everything on your shopping list. Ⓦ www.carrefour.es

HiperCor Owned by El Corte Inglés, Spain's largest department store, this chain not only features numerous Madrid locations but also an online shopping and delivery service. Ⓦ www.hipercor.es

EL RASTRO

Like digging for treasures? You'll find plenty of them—for cheap—at El Rastro, Madrid's famous Sunday flea market. It runs through the streets between La Latina and Lavapiés and packs in thousands of people on narrow streets and plazas. Here you can buy everything you could possibly want or need: antiques, cheap jewelry, T-shirts, luggage, old spoons, and personal items sold on blankets. El Rastro is so popular that it's wise to avoid peak hours (12:00 P.M. to 2:00 P.M.) to save your sanity. At the very least, keep a close eye on your wallet or purse, as petty theft is extremely common. Hours are from 10:00 A.M. 'til about 3:00 P.M. Ⓜ La Latina

HOME FURNISHINGS

If you're moving into an unfurnished apartment, or if you want to change your décor, take heart: There are not one but *two* gargantuan IKEA warehouses in Madrid. One lies in the northern neighborhood of San Sebastian de los Reyes, the other in the southern area of Alcorcón. Both can be reached by public transportation. On the higher end of the spectrum are shops such as Habitat, which sells trendy modern designs, and Tu Mueble, a Spanish chain that offers traditional designs at affordable prices.

Of course, Madrid also offers an option even cheaper than IKEA: the street! Every few months, Madrid invites its residents to throw out any furniture they no longer want, which is then yours for the picking. Look for posters in your neighborhood announcing the *recogida gratuita de muebles y trastos viejos* (free old furniture).

IKEA (San Sebastian de los Reyes) ⒜ Plaza del Comercio, 1 Megapark, ⓣ 902 400 922, ⓦ www.ikea.com, Bus #156, leaving from Plaza Castilla

IKEA (Alcorcón) ⒜ Av. Europa 22, ⓣ 902 400 922 ⓦ www.ikea.com, Ⓜ Parque Oeste

Habitat ⒜ Paseo de la Castellana 79, ⓣ 91 555 34 54, Ⓜ Nuevos Ministerios; ⒜ C/ Hermosilla 18, ⓣ 91 181 26 00, ⓦ www.habitat.net, Ⓜ Goya

Tu Mueble ⒜ C/ Alberto Aguilera 32, ⓣ 91 593 13 37, ⓦ www.tumueble.com, Ⓜ Argüelles

HIGH-TRAFFIC SHOPPING AREAS

Part of the fun of living in Madrid is discovering the amazing shops that seem to lurk around every corner and getting to know the unique stores that are closest to your home or school. If you're in the mood for a shopping spree, head to one of these neighborhoods, each of which offers a staggering shopping selection:

Argüelles/Moncloa This neighborhood's Calle Princesa is lined with luxury shops selling clothes, shoes, and gifts, in addition to bookstores catering to the Ciudad Universitaria student community. Ⓜ Argüelles, Ventura Rodríguez

Gran Vía The major commercial artery in Madrid, Gran Vía, is home to hotels; movie theaters; brand-name clothing stores such as Zara, Pull & Bear, and H&M; Spain's massive department store El Corte Inglés; and the French music and book emporium, Fnac. Ⓜ Gran Vía

Salamanca Salamanca is the heart of high-fashion Madrid. Here you'll find designer boutiques—from Armani, Louis Vuitton, and Prada to Spanish shops Adolfo Dominguez and Loewe—and *centros comerciales* (shopping malls) such as ABC Serrano, El Jardín de Serrano, Serrano 88, and Moda Shopping. Ⓜ Rubén Darío

Puerta del Sol Sol is packed with department stores (including three branches of El Corte Inglés and a Fnac), trendy brand-name clothing stores such as Top Shop and Zara, and souvenir shops. Ⓜ Sol

Chueca A little less expensive than its northern neighbor Salamanca, Chueca is decidedly funkier, with younger designers who sell hip, unique merchandise. Chueca's Mercado Fuencarral is an indoor minimall, with three floors of shops selling urban streetwear, accessories, music, and furniture. This is also the place to get a tattoo or a piercing. Ⓜ Chueca

5 GREAT GIFTS FOR
PEOPLE BACK HOME

1. **Castinettes:** These are the traditional hand-clappers used during flamenco performances. Whether you dance or not, they make for fun, easy-to-transport souvenirs.

2. **Olives:** More delicious than those in the United States, Spanish olives come in cans rather than jars, which makes for lighter and less risky packing.

3. **Scarves:** Spaniards have a thing for beautiful scarves—they're considered a wardrobe staple. Choose from expensive silk and cashmere or dig for hip and colorful (and sometimes cheaper) selections at El Rastro, Madrid's Sunday flea market. Ⓜ La Latina

4. **Sherry:** Authentic sherry, Spain's most celebrated export, comes from only one place in Spain: the city of Jerez de la Frontera in Andalusia. You can choose from a range of flavors, from dry and salty to sweet and dark.

5. **Turron:** A delicious, nougat-like confection made mostly from crushed nuts and sugar, turron comes in both soft and hard versions and is deliciously addictive. Although it's considered a Christmas candy, you can buy turron year-round at any big bakery.

6. Daily Living

Learning to navigate the ins and outs of daily life is part of the game when you're assimilating to any new city. Skills that you take for granted, such as how to do laundry, handle money matters, and mail packages, will suddenly seem new and perplexing. Factor in the linguistic barrier, and even the simplest tasks will become enormous—and often comical—new challenges.

Madrid is a great place for meeting people and enjoying yourself; however, it's not a great place for getting things done. In almost every situation, Madrileños will be in less of a hurry than you are. Planning in advance—and remaining flexible—will ensure that you're not left high and dry. It's all part of living daily life in Madrid, so try to keep your senses of humor and adventure.

GETTING MONEY

Before you leave home, set up your U.S. bank and credit card accounts to make them easier to manage from outside the country. Make a point of signing up for online banking and electronic bill payment. Notify your debit- and credit-card providers that you'll be using your cards overseas. Finally, find out how to deposit checks by mail because you won't be able to make deposits to U.S. bank accounts from ATMs in Madrid.

GETTING CASH FROM HOME

The fastest and most economical way to get cash from home is to withdraw it from your U.S. account through an ATM. Most U.S. banks place daily (and often weekly) withdrawal limits and charge transaction and currency conversion fees. Check with your bank for details. Also keep in mind the following options:

- **Cash advance on your credit card:** You can pull cash from your credit card but, you'll need to make sure you have a personal identification number (PIN) before you leave the United States. Be warned: Interest rates can exceed 25 percent.

- **Cashing U.S. checks:** As a general rule, it's best not to have U.S. checks mailed to you, as you'll have a difficult time finding a bank in Madrid that will cash them. Your university might have a check-cashing program; inquire at your school.

- **International money transfers:** If you have a Spanish bank account, you can have money transferred into your account through an international money transfer. This can take up to forty-eight hours, and a moderate-to-steep fee is usually charged.

- **Western Union or American Express:** You'll receive money within about an hour using either of these services, but the fees are exorbitant. For the nearest locations in Madrid, go to www.westernunion.com or www.americanexpress.com.

- **Wiring money:** You can arrange to have money wired to you from your U.S. bank, but both the sending and receiving banks charge fees, and the transfer can take up to ten business days or longer. This isn't a good choice if you need money quickly.

CHANGING MONEY

Unfortunately for U.S. travelers, the euro has been worth more than the dollar in recent years. The exchange rate fluctuates constantly, but the cost may vary from about $1.15 to $1.45 for one euro (you can easily locate the current exchange rate with a quick online currency search). If you're on a tight budget, check daily and wait until the rate is most favorable before withdrawing or exchanging a large sum of money. Using ATMs to withdraw cash is your best bet for getting a good exchange rate. Here are some other options for exchanging dollars for euros or vice versa:

- **Banks:** The headquarters of most large banks and some smaller branches in tourist areas will allow you to buy and sell dollars and euros, but regular neighborhood bank branches will not.

- **Airports:** You'll notice booths at the airports, both when you leave the United States and when you arrive in Madrid. Generally, these booths offer very unfavorable rates.

- **Exchange counters:** Currency-conversion kiosks are located at train stations and in touristy areas, such as Gran Vía and Sol; expect to be charged a high commission.

CREDIT CARDS

MasterCard and Visa are widely accepted in Spain. If you're an American Express user, bring a back-up card because Amex is not consistently recognized in Europe. Before you leave the United States, call your credit card companies and let them know you'll be abroad to prevent false alarms about fraudulent charges. Also ask about what fees you may be charged for overseas transactions; the industry standard is a 2- to 3-percent finance charge.

SPANISH BANK ACCOUNTS

It might be possible to get by without opening a bank account in Madrid—at least for a short period of time (six months or less). But if you'll be living in Madrid for longer than that, opening a Spanish bank account is probably a good idea. Having a Spanish account will allow you to deposit in euro checks you receive in dollars and avoid charges assessed by U.S. banks for overseas transactions. And if plan to live on your own in an apartment, you'll usually need to have a local bank account to sign up for utilities (see "Apartment Living").

OPENING AN ACCOUNT

Your school may have a partnership with a branch of a specific bank, an option worth checking out. If you need to select a bank on your own, you'll find that there is no consensus as to which bank offers the best service. There are two basic accounts: a *cuenta de ahorros* (savings account) or a *cuenta corriente* (checking account). Many banks offer "youth" advantages for people in their early twenties. Choose a bank that's located near where you live or study. Although you can make withdrawals and deposits at any branch of your bank in the city, all paperwork must be completed at your home bank, which is the branch where you opened your account. Most banks are open from 8:00 A.M. to 2:00 P.M. Monday through Friday, remaining open on Saturdays throughout fall and winter. Here are some of the most popular banks in Madrid; call or check their websites to find the nearest locations:

- **Banco Popular** Ⓦ www.bancopopular.es
- **BBVA (Banco Bilbao Vizcaya Argentaria)** Ⓦ www.bbva.es

- **BSCH (Banco Santander Central Hispano)**
  Ⓦ www.gruposantander.es
- **La Caixa** Ⓦ www.lacaixa.es
- **Caja Madrid** Ⓦ www.cajamadrid.es

ACCOUNT CHECKLIST

Bring the following with you when you apply to open a Spanish bank account:

- ✓ Passport
- ✓ Nonresident card, which you can apply for at local police headquarters
- ✓ Proof of residence
- ✓ Cash for your deposit

USING SPANISH CHECKS

You'll use Spanish checks with about the same frequency that you're used to back home—probably not often. Most utility bills are deducted automatically from your bank account, and most landlords deduct the rent automatically as well, rendering check writing virtually unnecessary.

POSTAL SERVICES

Correos, the Spanish postal system, has offices all around the city, with its headquarters in the magnificent edifice in the Plaza de Cibeles. Most offices are open from 8:30 A.M. to 8:30 P.M. Monday through Friday and from 8:30 A.M. to 1:30 P.M. on Saturdays. If a package is delivered to your apartment when you're not home, you'll receive a note telling you where you can pick it up. Be aware that postal workers won't leave correspondence in an unmarked mailbox—you must put your name on the exterior of your mailbox to receive mail.

A letter sent from Madrid to the United States, or visa versa, usually takes about ten days to arrive and will cost about €0.78. Unfortunately, there are no cheap options for sending packages; all companies charge by the kilo. If you send a package by Correos to the United States using the "economical" method, you'll pay €12.50 plus €4.50 per kilo; package delivery times are ambiguous (and can take up to six months to arrive), so sending them this way is not recommended. Sending packages "priority" (there's no real guarantee about what that means in Spain) will cost €18 plus €8 per kilo. A more reliable way to send a package is by a company such as UPS, which charges more than €200 for 7kg. For details on locations and hours of specific Correos branches, visit www.correos.es.

EXPRESS DELIVERY

If you need to get a package home fast, the following overseas shipping services are available:

- **DHL** Ⓦwww.dhl.es
- **Federal Express** Ⓦwww.fedex.com/es
- **Nacex** Ⓦwww.nacex.es
- **Seur** Ⓦwww.seur.com
- **UPS** Ⓦwww.ups.com

APARTMENT LIVING

As is the case back home, living in an apartment on your own presents many pleasures—along with many responsibilities. You'll have to pay for utilities, which are often in your landlord's name, in addition to rent. In general, utility bills are calculated every two months. If utilities are in your name, they'll be automatically deducted from your Spanish bank account. Here's a quick overview of utilities, services, and other day-in/day-out practicalities that are part of apartment living.

UTILITIES

- **Cable television:** Until recently, Madrid's only cable provider was Canal + (www.plus.es). Since then, the competition has expanded generously. In addition to Digital + (digital cable provided by Canal +), Auna-Cable (www.auna.es) and Telefónica's Imagenio (www.telefonica.es/imagenio.html) offer cable service. With cable, you'll generally get about forty channels. Some providers offer combined telephone/Internet/cable TV packages at discounted rates. Check out the companies' websites for prices and package options. For an overview of Spain's television and radio stations, see "TV and Radio Stations" in Chapter 7.

- **Electricity:** Electricity rates are moderate; however, the summertime use of an air conditioner, if you're lucky enough to have one, or the use of electric heaters in winter can drastically increase costs. Service will already be turned on when you enter into a rental agreement, and the account will typically be in the name of your landlord. If this is the case, you'll pay your landlord for electricity after he or she pays the bill, just as with other utilities. For more information, go to the website of Iberdrola, Spain's leading private electric company: www.iberdrola.es.

- **Gas:** Most apartments in Madrid have a boiler that regulates the natural gas that heats the water and lights the stove; however, some apartments require butane tanks for their gas supply. Ask any potential landlord to explain an apartment's gas situation before you sign a lease. Occasionally, you'll be able to control your apartment's heating system, but in most buildings, a central boiler supplies heat to every apartment. In this case, heat will come free with your rent, but you may not have direct control over the temperature. These gas systems are controlled by Gas Natural (www.gasnatural.com).

- **Internet service:** If you want Internet service hooked up in your apartment, you have several options: You can get cable Internet through Auna (www.auna.es) or a high-speed connection via an electrical outlet through Iberdrola (www.iberdrola. es). However, the most popular option is ADSL, or high-speed Internet via a telephone line. Before you can install ADSL, you'll need to turn on telephone service in your apartment (see "Landlines" for details). Wanadoo (www.wanadoo.es), Ya (www. ya.com), and Telefónica (www.telefonica.es) are among the most popular ADSL providers.

- **Telephones:** Having a landline in Madrid is generally viewed as a convenience, not a necessity, but it's imperative if you want Internet service at home. Your landline service will almost always be provided by Telefónica (www.telefonicaonline.com). To get a landline connected, call 1004, Telefónica's toll-free number, or 900 555 022. The line connection fee can cost up to €60, and bills (sent out every two months) include fees for line maintenance, regardless of the calls you make. Telefónica's line charge is €14 a month, regardless of the calling plan you have. If you want to use a company besides Telefónica for your calls and Internet service once you have a landline installed, your options include

Ya and Wanadoo (see "Internet service"). Telefónica's only major competitor for landline service is Jazztel (www.jazztel.es), which offers a variety of low-cost plans (call 1567 toll-free from a landline phone or 902 946 946).

- **Water:** Not all apartment rentals will require that you pay for water. It's often included in the *comunidad* (common building expenses shared by all the tenants). If you do have to pay for personal water usage, unlike other utilities that bill every two months, the local water department tends to bill quarterly.

SERVICES

- **Garbage:** Garbage collectors make their rounds nightly. If you live in a building without a doorman, you'll have to deposit your trash yourself in the orange-and-gray containers on the sidewalk. If you live in a doorman building, you have it easier: Leave your garbage in small bags in the hall outside your apartment door, and your doorman will collect it every night at around 8:00 P.M.

- **Locksmiths:** If you find yourself locked out of your apartment, there are locksmiths in every neighborhood, and twenty-four-hour locksmiths are advertised in the *Paginas Amarillas* (Yellow Pages) www.paginasamarillas.es. Having your locks replaced can cost anywhere from €70 to €130.

- **Maintenance:** If anything should go wrong in your apartment, call your landlord immediately. Before renting an apartment, ask the landlord whether the building is insured; if it is, your landlord is responsible for paying for needed work. However, although you likely won't have to pay, you may be required to schedule the necessary appointments. Always ask for an estimate of the work to be done so that you can alert your landlord and avoid any surprises.

- **Recycling:** Not all apartment buildings in Madrid recycle materials: You can tell whether your building recycles if there is a yellow bin (for plastics and metals only) placed outside the front door of your building every night. If you're lucky enough to have a doorman who picks up your garbage, you'll need only to separate organic trash from plastics and metals. To recycle paper and glass, bring your recyclables to one of the brown gumdrop-shaped containers located a few blocks apart all over the city. They're usually placed in groups of two: *vidrio* (glass) and *papel y cartón* (paper and cardboard).

PRACTICALITIES

- **Converters and adaptors:** In Spain, as in most European countries, the standard outlet carries 220–240 volts (compared to a standard of 110–120 volts in the United States). Plugs are shaped differently as well. If you want to bring (and use) your favorite hair dryer or other electric device from home, you'll need to buy a plug adaptor or voltage adaptor/converter before you leave. Plug adaptors will allow dual-voltage appliances (such as most laptops) to be plugged in, but they don't actually convert electricity. Voltage converters enable you to run small electric appliances intended for short periods of time. Voltage transformers—sold in kits for about $30—let you use your larger appliances, such as CD players or TVs.

- **Laundry and dry cleaning:** Nearly all of Madrid's furnished apartments have washing machines in their kitchens, rendering laundromats virtually unnecessary. You may be able to find a few across the city, but they're certainly few and far between. On the flip side, you'll rarely find a home with a clothes dryer. Madrid's climate is extremely dry, which makes air-drying wet clothes easy. All you need is a folding clothes rack, or you can hang laundry on the clotheslines that often run across the interior patios of buildings. And for your nicer clothes, there's at least one *tintorería* (dry cleaner) in every neighborhood in Madrid. Dry cleaning is expensive: Expect to pay about €3 for shirts; €4 for sweaters, slacks, and dresses; €5 for sport jackets; and €9 for coats.

5 AFFORDABLE CITY ADVENTURES

1. **Parque de Atracciones:** Hit Madrid's amusement park at Casa de Campo, which has the familiar roster of roller coasters and other rides. Admission is just €4.50, and individual rides cost €1.50. Ⓐ Casa de Campo, Ⓣ 91 463 29 00, Ⓦ www.parquedeatracciones.es, Ⓜ Batán

2. **Parque Zoologico:** Madrid's zoo is by no means a kids-only zone. Check out its more than 2,000 animals, representing 500 species—as well as the cool aquarium—for €13. Ⓐ Casa de Campo, Ⓣ 91 512 37 70, Ⓦ www.zoomadrid.com, Ⓜ Batán

3. **El Rastro:** You'll never lack for adventure at El Rastro, the oldest and most famous flea market in Madrid. You can wade through the crowds and merchandise-laden tables every Sunday. Ⓐ Calle de la Ribera de Curtidores, Ⓜ La Latina, Puerta de Toledo, Tirso de Molina

4. **Rowboats at Retiro:** At only €5 a boat for up to three people, renting a rowboat at Parque de Buen Retiro is a cheap thrill that you shouldn't miss. The park's manmade lake may feel a little like a fishbowl, but you'll be surprised at how much fun it is to row around. Ⓜ Retiro

5. **The Teleférico:** One of the coolest ways to see Madrid, the cable railway Teleférico goes from the Parque del Oeste to Casa de Campo (both on the west side of the city) and offers excellent views of Palacio Real and the Basilica de San Francisco el Grande. A round-trip ticket is just €4.10. Ⓣ 91 541 74 50, Ⓦ www.teleferico.com, Ⓜ Argüelles

7. Studying & Staying Informed

You'll find no shortage of quiet spots in Madrid where you can hit the books—while still feeling like you're close to the city's action. The free and user-friendly public libraries warrant exploration, and you'll find a host of other options as well.

Embracing the media in Madrid will enrich your experience in the city immensely, and exploring various news publications will help you to hold your own in a discussion with neighbors about Spanish politics or the latest soccer-match intrigue. When you feel the need to get in touch with your American roots, you'll find plenty of English-language bookstores for browsing.

PLACES TO STUDY

It can be difficult to study in a city as fun and lively as Madrid. But when you do hit the books, there's no need to shut yourself up in your apartment or dorm room: Madrid offers excellent spots that might take some of the sting out of studying. Here are a few good choices:

Diurno Tthis cool cafe has free wi-fi and doubles as a video store. There are a lot of tables and chairs, and the soundtrack is always low-key. But beware: Smoking is allowed, and patrons take advantage of it. Ⓐ Corner of C/ Libertad and San Marcos, Ⓣ 91 522 00 09, Ⓜ Chueco

Espresso Republic This chain is hugely popular with American students, most of whom trickle in from the international institute right down the street. The cafe has a "hidden" basement that's a haven for studying. Ⓐ C/ Miguel Angel 18, Ⓣ 91 319 84 10, Ⓜ Ruben Dario or Gregorio Marañon

Starbucks There are many Starbucks in Madrid, and almost all of them have free wi-fi. Some, such as the one on at C/ Serrano 41 (Ⓜ Serrano), have special basement rooms designed for studying.

Parque de Buen Retiro When the weather's nice—which it often is in Madrid—you can't beat Retiro as a studying destination. Flocks of students spread blankets on the grass and break out their books, sunbathing and learning simultaneously. Ⓜ Retiro

LIBRARIES

When it comes to your resource needs, your best bet is to stick with a university library. In the Complutense University, each *facultad* (college) has its own library with Internet access. Though these facilities are for students, IDs are rarely checked. The Complutense's Facultad de Ciencias de la Informacion (Ⓜ Ciudad Universitaria) also has a video library where anyone can watch a DVD or video free of charge.

REGIONAL AND MUNICIPAL LIBRARIES

There are nearly 200 public libraries throughout the Madrid area. A library card—acquired at any branch—gets you access to all branches, but you don't need a card just to visit or study. Be warned that the English-language sections will be small at best. Libraries also offer cultural activities and lectures—check your local branch for listings. More information is available at gestiona.madrid.org/bpcm for regional libraries and www.munimadrid.es/bibliotecaspublicas for municipal libraries. Here are two of Madrid's best libraries for studying:

- **Biblioteca del Instituto de Cooperacion Iberoamericana** Ⓐ Avda. De los Reyes Catolicos 4, Ⓣ 91 583 81 00, Ⓜ Moncloa
- **Biblioteca del Ateneo** Ⓐ C/ Prado 21, Ⓣ 91 429 17 50, Ⓜ Sevilla

THE NATIONAL LIBRARY

Biblioteca Nacional de España, a huge building in the Plaza de Colón, has the most extensive archives in the country. The facilities are accessible with a regular library card, but withdrawals are not permitted. Older archives are accessible only to those with a special researcher's card, for which you have to apply.

• **Biblioteca Nacional de España** Ⓐ Passeo de Recoletos 20–22, Ⓣ 91 580 78 00, Ⓦ www.bne.es, Ⓜ Colón

ENGLISH-LANGUAGE BOOKSTORES

To find books in English, visit any of the large, international bookstores such as Casa del Libro, Fnac, and Pasajes. Your other choice is to visit one of the city's specialized secondhand bookstores. Although these vendors aren't ideal if you're looking for a specific title, they're cheap and offer a random assortment of titles that you may not be able to find on the shelves of larger booksellers. Spend an afternoon perusing the offerings at the following stores:

Casa del Libro The closest thing Spain has to a Barnes & Noble, Casa del Libro has a decent English-language section, and you'll usually be able to find even the newest fiction from the United States. Ⓐ Various locations, Ⓣ 90 202 64 03, Ⓦ www.casadellibro.es

Fnac A media superstore, this Madrid landmark has five floors of magazines, books, music, movies, and electronics. Prices tend to be high for English-language books, but it has a good selection, particularly for fiction and travel guides. Ⓐ C/ Preciados 28, Ⓣ 91 595 61 00, Ⓦ www.fnac.es, Ⓜ Callao

J & J Books and Coffee With a small cafe/bar on the main level and stacks of English-language books downstairs, you could easily camp out at this used bookstore for hours. The shop offers a daily happy hour (4:00 P.M. to 7:00 P.M.) and open *intercambios* (language exchanges) in which English speakers and Spanish speakers meet to improve their conversation skills every weeknight after 8:00 P.M. Ⓐ C/ Espiritu Santo 47, Ⓣ 91 521 82 56, Ⓦ www.jandjbooksandcoffee.net, Ⓜ Noviciado

La Librería de Lavapiés This small, homey bookshop and stationery store is worth a visit, both for its great selection and for its cool ambiance. Ⓐ C/ Argumosa 39, Ⓣ 91 527 89 92, Ⓦ www.lalibreriadelavapies.com, Ⓜ Lavapiés

Pasajes This international bookstore has a good selection of contemporary and classic literature in English on its lower level. If Pasajes doesn't stock what you're looking for, it has a book-order service for hard-to-find texts. Ⓐ C/ Genova 3, Ⓣ 91 310 12 45, Ⓦ www.pasajeslibros.com, Ⓜ Alonso Martínez

Petra's International Bookshop This bookstore is cozy and cluttered and has an eclectic assortment of international books in their original languages. Petra's is known as a good meeting place for *intercambios*. Ⓐ C/ Campomanes 13, Ⓣ 91 541 72 91, Ⓜ Santo Domingo

NEWSPAPERS

Periodicals are big business in Madrid. You can't walk more than two blocks without passing a kiosk, bookstore, or cafe with an ample selection of the day's papers. Most daily newspapers cost about €1, which may seem a tad expensive but is justified by the limits placed on advertisements. Here are some of the major Spanish newspapers:

El País One of the most left-leaning Spanish newspapers, *El País* has a great travel section every Saturday. Ⓦ www.elpais.com

El Mundo One of Spain's largest daily newspapers, planted firmly on the liberal side of the political spectrum. Ⓦ www.elmundo.es

ABC Madrid's oldest newspaper, founded in 1903 and a favorite of conservative readers. Ⓦ www.abc.es

La Razón A leading conservative newspaper with editions in several Spanish cities. Ⓦ www.larazon.es

Marca Madrid's top-selling daily sports newspaper. Ⓦ www.marca.com

As Another sports daily that, like *Marca,* covers Real Madrid—the soccer team—in excruciatingly close detail. Ⓦ www.as.com

FREE NEWSPAPERS

Madrid offers a wide selection of free daily papers. *20 Minutos* (www.20minutos.es) and *Metro* (www.metrodirecto.com) are the flag-bearers, handed out every morning in various metro stations and on street corners and left on metal stands inside some cafes and bars. *Que!* (www.quediario.com) and *ADN* (www.diarioadn.com) are new additions to the free-paper mix, as well as the sports dailies *Penalty* and *Crack 10.*

NEWSPAPERS IN ENGLISH

If you're aching for an English-language newspaper, your best bet is to check out the online version of your favorite paper from home. The *International Herald Tribune* (www.iht.com) is also available at any newsstand. You'll also find *USA Today* at most kiosks, as well as the British newspapers the *Times* and the *Financial Times.* A free local English-language monthly paper called *InMadrid* (www.in-madrid.com) can be found in places frequented by foreign visitors; in addition to articles about cultural events in Madrid, it features classified sections for apartment rentals, personals, and services.

MAGAZINES

Madrileños love gossip rags, and these are the most visible magazines spread on shelves and racks at kiosks throughout the city. If you want a taste of home, many popular magazines publish Spanish versions, and you can usually find English-language editions at the media superstore Fnac and at the 7-Eleven-like VIPS stores located all over the city. The following are worth noting:

Hola! and *Que Me Dices!* Popular weekly gossip magazines featuring Spanish and European celebrities, along with the occasional big-name American star. Ⓦ www.hola.com, Ⓦ www.quemedices.orange.es

Muy Interesante A monthly periodical that centers around science- and history-related topics, diverse enough to analyze the Wild West one week and the blue whale the next. Ⓦ www.muyinteresante.es

Que Leer A serious, intellectual magazine dedicated mainly to classic and contemporary literature. It includes news articles, interviews, and reviews. Ⓦ www.que-leer.orange.es

TV AND RADIO

Everything happens later in Spain than in the United States, and television scheduling is no exception. The *telediarios* (Spain's version of the six o'clock news) are an hour long, uninterrupted by commercials, and air at 3:00 P.M. and 9:00 P.M. daily. Primetime TV hours are 10:00 P.M. to 1:00 A.M. Even Saturday night soccer matches—one of which is always shown on Telemadrid—begin at 10:00 P.M.

While the number of cable-ready homes is steadily growing, most TVs in Madrid carry no more than six or seven channels. These offer a similar mix of programming, which includes daytime talk shows, films, game shows, and sitcoms. They also carry Spanish-dubbed versions of some popular American shows. Here is a selection of popular Spanish television and radio stations:

TVE-1 and TVE-2 (Televisión Española 1 and 2) These public channels are owned and operated by the Spanish government.

Telemadrid This public channel is run by Madrid's local government.

Antena-3, Telecinco, Cuatro, and La Sexta Some of the major privately owned channels; the latter two are recent additions.

40 Principales (93.9) Spain's top 40 station, playing the newest hit songs by both Spanish and Latin American artists and English-speaking pop stars. ⓦ www.los40.com

Cadena Ser (94.4) Offers talk shows, news, and variety programs. It's one of the most listened-to stations in Spain. ⓦ www.cadenaser.com

Kiss FM (102.7) Plays popular '70s, '80s, '90s, and contemporary tracks from across the globe. ⓦ www.kissfm.es

Radio 3 (93.2) Plays more cutting-edge music and often features interviews with artists. It's one of a few national stations making up Radio Nacional Española (RNE), which is akin to NPR in the United States. ⓦ www.rtve.es/rne/r3

5 GOOD EXCUSES NOT TO STUDY

1. **Sunny Spanish weather:** They don't call Spain *el país del sol* (the country of sun) for nothing!

2. **Bars open for business at 8:00 A.M.:** Just the fact that you can order a cognac with breakfast is reason enough to shun your books for at least a few more hours.

3. **Do as the locals do:** Most Spanish students take six to eight years to finish their college degrees. If they're not in a rush, why should you be?

4. **The importance of language immersion:** Any Spanish-language teacher will tell you that the only way to speak better Spanish is to practice, practice, practice. Consider your cafe-sitting an academic activity: You'll learn more from talking to the natives than from doing your homework.

5. **Telenovelas:** Strategically scheduled during the afternoon lull, these Spanish soap operas are so over the top and ridiculous that you'll find yourself getting sucked in, even if you can't understand half the dialogue.

*02 Pulse

Compra aquí por 3€ el pin para llamar a tu país. Así de fácil. Así de rápido.

PULSA *01 PARA ENVIAR
S M S
E-MAIL
FAX

8. Staying in Touch

One of the most difficult aspects about moving to Madrid is being separated from family and friends. While homesickness is a normal part of studying abroad, luckily there are loads of opportunities to stay connected in real time to those near and dear to you. The Internet is the easiest and cheapest option—in fact, after a few weeks, you'll probably find yourself on a first-name basis with the proprietor of your neighborhood Internet cafe.

As in most places in the world, cell phones are ubiquitous in Madrid, and many who land in Madrid—even for short stays—find that getting set up with a Spanish phone and service is essential to feeling connected and like they're really a part of city life.

THE INTERNET

The easiest way to get online is probably through your university's computer lab. If you live in university housing, your dorm or apartment should be hooked up as well. When the computer labs are too crowded, you'll find Internet cafes and *locutorios*, which offer indoor pay phones for international calls and often Internet service as well, all over Madrid. An hour of service may cost €1 to €2; most places offer vouchers of five or ten hours. You should try out a few different places until you find one with agreeable rates and atmosphere. Madrid also has a variety of free wi-fi places. Here are some popular options for getting online:

Faborit This cafe offers free wireless service to customers.
Ⓐ C/ Alcalá 21, Ⓣ 91 522 11 06 Ⓜ Sevilla

Irish Rover Another cafe that provides free wireless service.
Ⓐ Avenida de Brasil 7, Ⓣ 91 597 48 11, Ⓜ Santiago Bernabeu

La Casa Encendida A public museum/exhibition center that has a computer room with free Internet access. ⒶC/ Ronda Valencia 2, Ⓣ 91 506 38 75, Ⓦ www.lacasaencendida.com, ⓂAtocha and Embajadores

Universidad Complutense Most colleges at this university have specified computer rooms, which are free for students. Most don't check for student IDs, although it can't hurt to bring yours.

CELL PHONES

With rare exceptions, cell phones purchased in the United States won't work in Europe. If you want to use a cell phone during your stay in Madrid, you'll most likely need to buy a Spanish cell phone and investigate Spain's various options for getting service.

USING RECHARGEABLE SIM CARDS

Pay-as-you-go SIM (or, subscriber identity module) cards are the best option if you'll be in Madrid for a short time. This is also your only option if you don't have a Spanish bank account or haven't opened one yet. With these microchips, or *tarjeta/prepago* (card/prepaid), you don't have to sign a contract with a cellular provider; you just slip the card (smaller than a postage stamp) into your phone and buy blocks of minutes as you need them. Available in denominations starting at about €25, the cards are sold at tabacco shops, supermarket checkout counters, and locutorios. They can be recharged with additional minutes as necessary. To use SIM cards, you'll need to purchase a Spanish cell phone, except in the rare case that your U.S. phone is SIM card–compatible (see "Using Your U.S. Cell Phone" later in this chapter).

WATCH YOUR PHONE!

The fact that SIM cards will work on any phone makes cell phones one of the most commonly stolen items in Madrid. Leaving yours on a cafe table, in a see-through pocket of your knapsack, or even in your hand while walking down a busy street is a risk. On the other hand, SIM cards also mean that should your phone break, your address book will be intact.

SIGNING A CONTRACT

If you plan to stay in Spain for a long time, consider signing up with a Spanish provider. There are several Spanish service providers, all of which provide comparable rates and contract lengths, which normally require at least a one-year commitment. Do some serious comparison shopping to find the best deal, and find out whether your university offers special deals through any company. Your plan will often include options such as flat rates at certain hours of the day and extremely low rates to the number you call most frequently. Here are your service provider options:

- Amena ⓦ www.amena.com
- Movistar (Telefónica) ⓦ www.movistar.com
- Vodafone ⓦ www.vodafone.es

USING YOUR U.S. CELL PHONE

It may be possible for you to use your U.S. cell phone during your time in Madrid. First, you'll need to make sure that your phone is "multiband"; contact your U.S. service provider for more information. If your phone is indeed multiband, you can sign up for international roaming. However, be forewarned: While convenient, international roaming is very expensive and can result in astronomical phone bills. A more affordable option is to switch your phone over to a Spanish calling plan. To do this, you'll need to ask your U.S. service provider to unlock your phone, which allows it to work on other providers' networks.

TEXT MESSAGING, MADRID-STYLE

Texting is undoubtedly more popular in Madrid than it is in the United States. Words are frequently shortened, accent marks are cast aside, and punctuation is often completely ignored. After a couple of months in Madrid, you'll understand what that attractive Spaniard you just met last weekend is asking when you receive a text reading, "Q aces ste finde?" (*Que haces este fin de semana*, or "What are you doing this weekend?")

CALLING HOME

Rest assured, there are a number of affordable options for placing international calls, so your friends and folks back home won't forget the sound of your voice. But remember: Madrid is six hours ahead of the U.S. East Coast and nine hours ahead of the West Coast, so if you want to catch people when they're home from school or work and awake, you may have to stay up pretty late to do so. If you choose to buy a Spanish cell phone, all incoming calls are free—so do your best to convince your folks and friends back home to call you.

CALLING CARDS

Calling cards—which can be used from any cell phone, pay phone, or home phone—generally provide the best deals on international phone calls. A €5 or €6 card will give you anywhere from hundreds to thousands of minutes for calls abroad, but shop around. There are many types of calling cards in Spain, with prices depending on where you're calling to and the type of phone you're calling from. You'll find the cards for sale at tobacco shops, newsstands, Internet cafes and corner stores, as well as in all one-stop shopping locations, such as OpenCor or El Corte Inglés.

To use a Spanish calling card, you dial an access number, enter a password, and then dial the number of the phone you want to reach, including the country code. You'll find two access numbers on the card: If you choose the local number, you'll get more minutes but will have to pay for the local call; if you choose the toll-free number, you'll get fewer minutes but will save the cost of the local call. Calling cards typically expire within two months, so be sure to use the minutes you purchase within that time frame.

DIRECT CALLS

Placing direct calls from either cell phones or landlines is going to cost you more—use a calling card when calling home to avoid the exorbitant rates. Calls within Spain aren't qualified as local or long-distance, national, or international. Many landline plans offer national calls (within Spain) for one flat rate.

HOW TO DIAL INTERNATIONAL NUMBERS

Here's a quick guide to dialling international numbers from landlines. See the "Country Codes" list in the appendix for a list of commonly used country codes in Western Europe and North America.

- **Numbers in the United States** Dial 001 + area code + number. For example, dial 001 555 123 4567.
- **Numbers in other countries** Dial 00 + country code + city code + number. For example, dial 00 48 12 123 4567 (to reach someone in Krakow, Poland).

VOICE OVER IP

Voice over Internet Protocol (VoIP) is the most economical choice for making international calls. With it, you place your calls with a computer and a high-speed Internet connection. The cheapest and easiest way to make VoIP calls is to use the computer-to-computer method, which is free if your friends and family have the same equipment you do. Calls to people who do not have VoIP equipment still cost very little—usually less than €0.05/minute for connections to the United States.

To set yourself up to use VoIP, you'll need a headset—or you can use the speakers and microphone that come integrated with most new laptops. If you don't have these items already, a trip to PC City (www.pccity.es) or the *informatica* (computer technology) departments of any Fnac or El Corte Inglés will take care of things. Then, simply download the software from your chosen VoIP provider's website; it's probably best to stick to the big names, such as Vonage and Skype.

- **AIM (an America Online service)** Ⓦ www.aim.com
- **Google Talk** Ⓦ www.google.com/talk
- **Skype** Ⓦ www.skype.com
- **Vonage** Ⓦ www.vonage.com
- **Yahoo** Ⓦ www.yahoo.com

8 . STAYING IN TOUCH

PAYPHONES

You'll find payphones on street corners all over Madrid. Payphones accept coins and calling cards—look on the back of the card for your dial-ling options. Locuturios across the city also offer private telephone booths with flat rates to a variety of countries—calling the United States from one of these stores shouldn't cost more than €0.20 a minute.

5 THINGS THAT WILL MAKE YOUR FRIENDS BACK HOME JEALOUS

1. **Alcohol in grocery stores:** No need to make a special trip to the liquor store as you do in many places in the United States. Spain's markets are well-stocked with everything from beer to wine to hard alcohol and mixers, all at cheaper prices than in the United States.

2. **Siestas:** Not since kindergarten has it been socially acceptable to take an afternoon nap, so take advantage of it while you can.

3. **Cheap drinks:** At restaurants, house beer and wine are just as inexpensive as soda, about €2 to €3 a drink.

4. **Lazy weekend mornings:** Because clubs and bars don't fill up until after midnight in Madrid, most people don't stumble home until the wee hours. It's completely normal to wake up the next day around lunchtime—which in Spain means 2:00 P.M.

5. **Great public transportation:** You can reach any destination in Madrid by metro or bus, and you'll never wait longer than ten minutes for your ride.

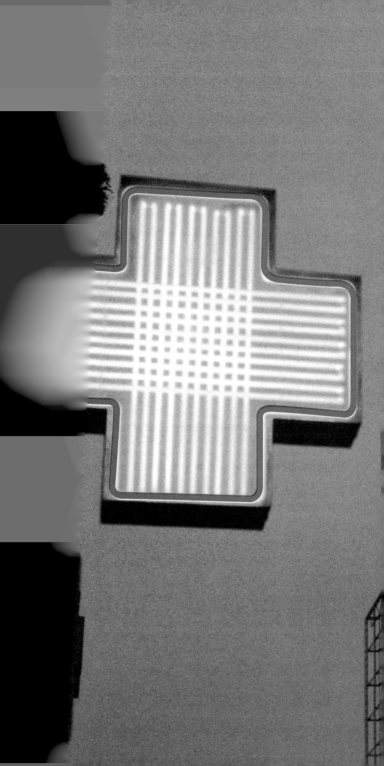

9. Health

Y ou must have adequate health insurance before you leave for Spain. You can't get a student visa without proof of insurance, and of course you'll want to be covered if you get sick or injured. Your school will most likely work with you to make sure you have an appropriate policy for your time in Madrid. But if, for whatever reason, your insurance situation is especially complicated, or if you think you may qualify to participate in Spain's state healthcare system, this chapter will help.

Rest assured that the doctors in Madrid are (in all likelihood) just as good as the doctors back home. Many of the Spanish physicians who participate in U.S. insurance plans are bilingual, so you should have no trouble finding an English-speaking doctor if you need one. Keep in mind, however, that the overwhelming majority of your medical encounters in Madrid, such as discussions with the local pharmacist, will be conducted in Spanish. For pertinent Spanish words and phrases see the "Useful Phrases" section in the appendix.

HEALTH INSURANCE

Most American insurance plans will reimburse you for your medical expenses, but they won't coordinate billing with European practices. In other words, you'll have to pay for all of your healthcare needs up front and out of pocket. This may sound daunting, but keep in mind that Spanish fees for doctor visits, procedures, and medicines are just a fraction of what they are back home—cost shouldn't stop you from seeking medical attention if you need it.

Private health insurance plans vary in what they cover. Before leaving for Spain, verify with your provider exactly what your policy entitles you to and make sure you understand every detail, requirement, and exclusion. Come prepared with your insurance card and claim forms every time you visit a pharmacy, doctor, or hospital. Keep your receipts so that you can get reimbursed. Your insurance company may require detailed forms and receipts translated into English, with euros converted into dollars.

THE SPANISH HEALTHCARE SYSTEM

All Spanish citizens and those paying social security taxes in Spain are entitled to benefit from Spain's public healthcare system, Instituto Nacional de la Salud (INSALUD). If you're eligible to receive benefits from INSALUD, you'll have free access to public doctors, though not necessarily a choice of physician or facility. Who else qualifies for coverage? Here are a few examples:

Who may be covered:

- Students enrolled directly in a Spanish university (as opposed to through an American study-abroad program)

- Employees of Spanish companies

- Spouses of Spanish citizens

Who will not be covered:

- Students enrolled in an American study-abroad program

- Students studying Spanish at a private language-instruction school

- Tourists

To receive your INSALUD *tarjeta sanitaria* (health

card) and to be assigned to a doctor, clinic, and hospital, you must be officially registered with the Instituto Nacional de Seguridad Social, Madrid's Social Security office. Required documentation will include your passport and proof of local residence.

• **Instito Nacional de Seguidad Social** Ⓐ Subdirección General de Relaciones Internacionales, Padre Damian 4, Ⓣ 91 564 76 81 or toll-free 900-166565, Ⓜ Cuzco

GETTING HEALTH COVERAGE

If you need health coverage (and you don't qualify for free Spanish coverage), here are a few insurance options:

- **Private Spanish insurance:** Private insurance plans in Spain are much cheaper than those offered in the United States, and services are comparable. Plans can cost anywhere from €40 to €100 a month, depending on your age, sex, and health as well as the type and amount of coverage offered— make sure your carrier explains exactly what you're entitled to. As a policyholder, you'll often be responsible for a copay or small fee, while the insurance carrier assumes the burden of the cost. Two carrier options are Sanitas (www.sanitas.es) and Asisa (www.asisa.es).

- **Global medical insurance:** Global medical insurance offers you coverage at home and abroad; find an insurer that offers individual policies.

- **Travel insurance:** Travel insurance policies typically include at least some level of medical and emergency coverage, and many even have specific policies designed for short-term residents of a country. They also provide twenty-four-hour travel assistance and coverage for trip cancellation, interruption, or delay, as well as lost or delayed baggage. Two reliable providers are Travel Guard International (www.travelguard.com) and Travel Insured International (www.travelinsured.com). You can compare various travel insurance companies at www.insuremytrip.com.

PHARMACIES

Unlike in the United States, a *farmacia*, or pharmacy—rather than a physician—should be your first stop when you're feeling under the weather. Pharmacists can give you an impromptu medical consultation and suggest medication. You may be surprised at the number of ailments they can help you with. Pharmacies are instantly recognizable by the neon-green crosses that hang above their entrances.

Typical pharmacy hours are 9:30 A.M. to 1:30 P.M. and 4:30 P.M. to 8:00 P.M. Monday through Saturday. However, there are plenty of *farmacias de guardia* (twenty-four-hour pharmacies) in Madrid. These pharmacies may seem vacant when you arrive at 6:00 A.M., but a pharmacist is always on duty; you just have to ring a doorbell to get services. Many pharmacists are aware of English translations of medical symptoms and generic medications. For more information on finding the twenty-four-hour pharmacy nearest you, call 098 toll-free from any telephone or visit the website www.canaldefarmacia.com. In addition, info on all-day, all-night pharmacies is posted in the windows of other pharmacies.

- Ⓐ C/ Atocha 46, Ⓜ Antón Martín, Atocha
- Ⓐ C/ Bailen 16, Ⓜ La Latina

- Ⓐ C/ Goya 12, Ⓜ Goya
- Ⓐ C/ Mayor 59, Ⓜ Sol, Opera
- Ⓐ C/ Velazquez 30, Ⓜ Velazquez

OVER-THE-COUNTER DRUGS

In Madrid, over-the-counter medications aren't displayed on shelves, so you'll need to explain your symptoms, however embarrassing, to the pharmacist. He or she can then get the medications you need from behind the counter. If you have a run-of-the-mill headache, cold, flu, or digestive problem (including diarrhea or constipation), you'll likely be able to get the medicine you need without a prescription. Remember that pharmacists know drugs by their generic names, as brand names differ by country. If you're looking for the Spanish equivalent of a particular American drug, bring your old bottle or package with you to show the pharmacist.

PRESCRIPTION DRUGS

For most antibiotics, birth control, or stronger drugs, pharmacists will require a *receta médica* (prescription). Prescription drugs in Spain are substantially less expensive than they are in the United States. Even if you're not covered by the Spanish public health system, it may be worthwhile to visit a physician when you arrive in Madrid in order to get a prescription for your American medications or their equivalents. This way you won't have to renew your prescriptions from across the Atlantic.

The public healthcare system covers essential medications that treat diseases such as cancer, as well as all medications for senior citizens. Most other prescription drugs are covered partially, with patients paying only about 30 percent of the cost. If you have a health card, feel free to address any doubts to your local pharmacist. If you have private health insurance, the coverage for prescription drugs can vary greatly. You'll need to consult your carrier and policy in order to determine the extent of your drug coverage.

VISITING THE DOCTOR

Fortunately, you'll have no problem finding an English-speaking doctor, dentist, or mental health professional in Madrid. For comprehensive listings of English-speaking health professionals in Madrid, visit the U.S. Embassy's website, madrid.usembassy.gov. Here's an overview of the different types of doctors you might see during your stay, as well as some advice on what to expect from your visits. For any appointment, be sure to check first with your insurance provider about the coverage you're entitled to and whom you're permitted to see.

- **Physicians:** While it's not difficult to find an English-speaking doctor in Madrid, be aware that the ones who are available may not fall under your insurance plan. Depending on your insurance situation, you may be assigned specific doctors and clinics according to your location within the city. All nonemergency medical attention will be directed to your assigned *atención primaria* (general practitioner). However, if your insurance plan offers more flexibility, you should be able to choose from a list of doctors, allowing you to find one who is bilingual.

- **Dentists:** Dental facilities may be less sterile-seeming than in the United States, but the quality of care is up to par. If you have private insurance, you'll likely be either partially or wholly reimbursed for whatever work you have done. The public health system generally covers only emergency dental care, so cleanings and cavity treatments will require full payment. Be forewarned: Dental care doesn't come cheap in Spain.

9. HEALTH

- **Ophthalmologists:** When it comes to getting new eyeglasses, you won't benefit from drastic savings in Spain. You won't be reimbursed for frames, but you may be partially reimbursed for your new lenses if you submit a written attestation to your insurance provider from your ophthalmologist stating that your prescription needs to be changed. Minimal vision care is provided under the public health system. Private carriers provide coverage, but check your policy for details.

- **Mental health professionals:** Therapy and psychoanalysis aren't nearly as common in Spain they are in the United States. Spanish public and private healthcare, however, are required by law to provide mental healthcare for those in need. Private insurance policies, of course, will vary in the extent of their coverage. Check with your carrier for details.

- **Gynecologists:** The protocol for a gynecological exam in Spain and the United States is similar, but be forewarned that paper gowns are not provided.

HOSPITALS/24-HOUR EMERGENCY ROOMS

Madrid has numerous hospitals and clinics, both public and private. In general, nearly anyone can receive medical attention at a public hospital. If you need emergency care, know that major hospitals all have emergency rooms (ERs). However, these ERs often have long wait times. Avoiding that long wait is the primary benefit of having private insurance and attending private clinics. The following public hospitals all have ERs:

Clínica Nuestra Señora de la Concepción (Fundación Jiménez Díaz) Ⓐ Avda. Reyes Católicos 2, Ⓣ 91 544 80 16, Ⓦ www.fjd.es, Ⓜ Moncloa

Hospital Gregorio Marañon Ⓐ C/ Doctor Esquerdo 46, Ⓣ 91 586 80 00, Ⓦ www.hggm.es, Ⓜ Sainz de Baranda, Odonnel, Ibiza

Hospital La Paz Ⓐ Paseo de la Castellana 261, Ⓣ 91 727 70 00, Ⓜ Plaza Castilla

Hospital de La Princesa Ⓐ C/ Diego de León 63, Ⓣ 91 520 22 00, Ⓜ Diego de León

SEXUAL HEALTH

To obtain birth-control pills in Madrid, you'll need a prescription. Or, consider getting your American doctor to prescribe a six-month or a one-year supply of birth-control pills and fill the prescriptions all at once. (If your insurance won't allow that, you can refill the prescription from Madrid and have the monthly packets sent to you.) The morning-after pill is available from pharmacies in Madrid with a prescription. It must be taken within seventy-two hours following unprotected sex to be effective.

In Spain, abortion is illegal except under certain conditions, such as if the pregnancy presents a danger to the patient's mental health. If doctors deem a woman in the early stages of pregnancy to be legally qualified to have an abortion, she can go to a private abortion clinic, such as Clínica Mayrit (www.clinicamayrit.com), which handles legal paperwork, provides support groups, and performs abortions at minimal or no cost. More information on abortion can be found at www.redmadres.org. Abortion is frequently referred to as an *interrupción voluntaria del embarazo,* or I.V.E. (voluntary pregnancy interruption).

SEXUAL HEALTH CLINICS

There are numerous sexual health clinics in Madrid that provide gynecological exams, pregnancy tests, condoms, emergency contraception, and birth control prescriptions, all free of charge. Bring a Spanish speaker with you if you need a translator, as you won't be guaranteed an English-speaking provider.

CMS Joven Ⓐ C/ Navas de Tolosa 101, Ⓣ 91 588 96 60, Ⓜ Sol

Centro Joven de Anticoncepción y Sexualidad Ⓐ C/ San Vicente Ferrer 86, Ⓣ 91 531 66 55, Ⓦ www.centrojoven.org, Ⓜ Noviciado

5 IDEAS FOR CONQUERING HOMESICKNESS

1. **American groceries:** Make a trip to the grocery store Taste of America for American brands such as Hershey's, Newman's Own, and Pepperidge Farm, which regular Spanish stores don't carry. Ⓐ C/ Serrano 149, Ⓣ 91 562 16 32, Ⓜ República Argentina

2. **American movies:** Take in an American film in v.o.s. (English with Spanish subtitles). See what's showing at the theatre Yelmo Cineplex Ideal Ⓐ C/Doctor Cortezo 6, Ⓣ 90 222 09 22, Ⓜ Tirso de Molina or Ⓜ Sol

3. **American publications:** It may be a splurge at €6 or so, but *People* magazine (the American—not the Spanish-language version) just hits the spot when you want to feel close to home. The newsstands around Sol and Retiro usually have the best selection of American publications.

4. **American burgers:** Nothing eases American food cravings like a juicy hamburger, and the hamburgers at the nearest VIPS fit the bill. Ⓦ www.vips.com

5. **American sports:** For the sporty comforts of home, watch an American football game at an Irish pub. Many Irish pubs advertise American sporting events.

10. Getting Involved

Moving beyond your student horizons can take some effort. While your schoolwork will probably be your first priority, you should make the most of your time by getting involved in life outside of school (schedule permitting, of course). You'll find endless opportunities to do so in Madrid, whether you're conducting scientific research through an internship, serving espresso at a cafe, or volunteering at a neighborhood hospital.

Once you settle into your new life, you may find that meeting locals is more challenging than befriending other foreign students and travelers—but it might just be that you're looking in the wrong places. You'll find scores of locals happy to meet foreigners at pubs and bars. Madrid's proximity to the rest of Europe helps create an open-mindedness regarding bilingual, binational, romantic, and platonic relationships.

MEETING LOCALS

It sounds like a study-abroad cliché, but making an effort to befriend Madrileños should be a requirement during your time in Madrid. Locals are excellent sources of practical and personal insight into the city, and the relationships you develop with them, whether they include the neighborhood newspaper vendor, the owner of the corner bar, or the chain-smoking guy in your art history class, will give you knowledge that would be impossible to gain hanging out with just Americans.

WHERE TO MEET MADRILEÑOS

Your university is the most obvious place to start your pursuit of Madrileño friendships, whether you're lingering in the halls during breaks between classes, getting involved in extracurricular activities, or taking extracurricular classes. Here are some ideas for making friends, both inside and outside of school:

- Join an intramural sports team or participate in a sports club (see Chapter 13, "Sports").

- Volunteer (see "Volunteer Opportunities").

- Go to a bar or club on a designated *intercambio* (language exchange) night. On Wednesdays, try J & J Books and Coffee (www.jandjbooksandcoffee.com).

- Sign up for a language class.

- Share an apartment with Spaniards (see "Homestays" in Chapter 4).

- On weekend nights, you'll find Spanish university students parading the streets of Moncloa, which is within walking distance of the Ciudad Universitaria metro stop. For a trendier scene, head to the Malasaña neighborhood.

LANGUAGE EXCHANGES

If you want to make a new Spanish friend, and bone up on your language skills at the same time, consider answering or posting an ad for an intercambio. During an intercambio, you and a native Spanish speaker meet for an hour or so to practice speaking both English and Spanish. You can find and post ads at your university or on websites such as www.descubremadrid.com.

DATING

Dating is considerably less formal in Spain than in the United States. The most common date consists of *quedar* (meeting up) to *tomar algo*, which translates roughly as "have something," be it tapas, drinks, coffee, or all of the above. If someone proposes that you tomar-algo together, it doesn't necessarily imply a romantic date: It just means that you'll go out and see what happens. Here are a few tips for navigating the dating world in Madrid:

- **Lateness:** Lateness is par for the course in Spain. Many Spaniards, especially females, tend to arrive fashionably late to all appointments. So if your date is tardy, don't take it as a lack of interest.

- **Machismo:** Some Spaniards retain certain ideals of *machismo* (or gallantry, depending on your perspective). If you're a woman on a date with a Spanish man, you can offer to help pay, but you'll probably be refused; if you're a man on a date with a Spanish woman, keep in mind when you plan the date that she may expect you to foot the bill.

- **Slow pace:** Romantic relationships with Spaniards generally take a while to develop. Young people often wait months before mentioning their significant others to their parents, let alone introducing them. This could impede romances between American students, who are in Madrid for a limited time, and Spanish locals.

- **Informality:** Many locals find American romantic customs too far-fetched and overdone. Rare is the Spaniard who gets down on one knee to propose, and elaborate anniversary or Valentine's Day celebrations are less common in Spain than they are in the United States.

CLUBS, ORGANIZATIONS, AND OTHER RESOURCES

Madrid has an enormous international student community and an astonishing array of social groups, including several groups that connect American and other foreign students. Before you leave you can check out groups' websites to access online message boards and newsletters—all of which can help answer questions about living in Madrid. Look for groups that provide services or events that match your interests, and be sure to check with your university about student groups. Many groups are informal and very local (often centered in particular neighborhoods), and you can locate them on bulletin boards at universities, libraries, international bookstores, and language schools.

EXPAT RESOURCES

Clubs and organizations are a great place to rub shoulders with Americans, and there are also a number of bars, bookstores, and other places that draw an American crowd. (For a list of English-language bookstores, see Chapter 7.) There's also a wide selection of expat resources that provide advice on everything from finding housing to finding new friends. You can start you investigation at websites such as www.spainexpat.com, www.expatriatecafe.com, and www.madridman.com, as well as these resources:

Easy Expat This website posts overseas job listings and information on finding healthcare, handling taxes, and locating apartments, schools, and volunteer opportunities. Ⓦ www.easyexpat.com

Expat Focus An online network with message boards, newsletters, and information for expats. Ⓦ www.expatfocus.com

Meetup This popular site gives international travelers a place to meet others with similar interests, swap travel experiences, and establish communities abroad. Ⓦ www.meetup.com

A Small World A European-based networking website that often hosts gatherings in cities around the world, including Madrid. It's a great way to meet young European students and recent graduates. Ⓦ www.asmallworld.net

Transitions Abroad A good source for information for study-abroad students, long-term travelers, and expats. Ⓦ www.transitionsabroad.com

MEETING INTERNATIONAL FRIENDS

Madrid is teeming with young Europeans. The city is also a popular destination for Spanish-speaking South Americans. Here are a few bars and cafes known for drawing students from all over the world:

Casa de la Cerveza The "House of Beer" is a bar that's very popular with international college students and other foreigners living in Madrid. Show your student ID, and you'll get 20 percent off drink prices from 10:30 P.M. to 1:30 A.M. Monday through Friday. Ⓐ Luchana 15, Ⓣ 91 447 37 84, Ⓜ Bilbao

Los Gabrieles A renowned student eating and drinking spot near Plaza del Sol. Ⓐ Echegaray 17, Ⓣ 91 429 62 61, Ⓜ Sevilla

Palacio Gaviria Thursday night at this club is international night, which is attended by foreigners who wear badges sporting their names and nationalities. Ⓐ C/ Arenal 9, Ⓣ 91 526 60 69, Ⓜ Sol

Viva Madrid A student and expat favorite that serves drinks, food, and coffee to an international student crowd. It features a full menu of cocktails as well as a variety of Spanish snacks, draft beer, and the ever-present *tinto* (red wine). Ⓐ Manuel Fernandez y Gonzalez 7, Ⓣ 91 429 36 40, Ⓦ www.barvivamadrid.com, Ⓜ Sevilla or Sol

VOLUNTEER OPPORTUNITIES

Volunteering is a great way to get involved in your local community—not to mention a great way to meet locals. The most obvious place to find volunteering opportunities is at your university, so look for signs on walls and bulletin boards. American universities with local campuses, such as Saint Louis University (spain.slu.edu), also promote local volunteer work. Here are a few places to contact:

Caritas Volunteering with this organization may put you side by side with the impoverished and needy. Caritas offers a training program for its volunteers. Ⓣ 91 548 95 80, Ⓦ www.caritas.es

Hacesfalta.org and La Plataforma del Volunariado These associations help coordinate volunteers; check out their websites to get in touch with local organizations. Hacesfalta.org allows you to specify an area in which to volunteer, such as free trade, human rights, education, or helping the disabled. Ⓦ www.hacesfalta.org, Ⓦ www.plataformavoluntariado.org

La Cruz Roja Espanola The Red Cross is an international organization providing medical assistance to those in need. Hands-on medical volunteers must submit to an interview and training period. Volunteers are also needed for administrative tasks. Ⓣ 91 532 55 55, Ⓦ www.cruzroja.es

Intermón Oxfam Assist this nongovernmental organization in fighting world poverty and hunger. Ⓣ 90 233 03 31, Ⓦ www.intermonoxfam.org

Voluntariado San Juan de Dios This organization's numerous medical facilities need volunteers to visit sick patients. Ⓣ 91 387 44 82, Ⓦ www.sanjuandedios-fjc.org

YMCA Madrid Most of the YMCA's volunteer opportunities are for supporting youth programs, from summer camps to after-school sessions. Ⓣ 91 319 21 26, Ⓦ www.ymcaesp.org

LGBT ORGANIZATIONS

There's no secret to meeting gays and lesbians in Madrid: Simply head to Chueca, the heart of the city's gay culture. For more information on gay life and events in Madrid, check out *Zero* (www.zero-web.com), the city's most visible gay publication.

Cogam An organization whose office in Chueca is a place to make friends. Ⓐ C/ Infantas 40, 1° dcha, Ⓣ 91 522 45 17, Ⓦ www.cogam.org, Ⓜ Chueca, Gran Vía

The Fundación Triángulo An organization dedicated to the gay and lesbian community; it sponsors events such as the annual Madrid Gay and Lesbian Film Festival (www.lesgaicinemad.com). Ⓐ C/ Eloy Gonzalo 25, 1° ext., Ⓣ 91 446 63 94, Ⓦ fundaciontriangulo.es/Madrid, Ⓜ Iglesia, Quevedo

5 *ALMOST* FREE WAYS TO IMPRESS YOUR DATE

1. **Rent a rowboat at Retiro:** There's something undeniably romantic about a rowboat ride, and the lake in the center of Parque del Buen Retiro provides the perfect setting. Rental prices for boats are cheap (€5 a boat for up to three people), leaving you some euros for wining and dining. Ⓜ Retiro

2. **Hit the Botanical Gardens:** These beautiful, extensive gardens next to the Museo de Prado are in bloom from March through November. With student discount prices at €2, it's well worth the price of admission. Ⓐ C/ Plaza de Murillo 2, Ⓜ Atocha

3. **Jazz it up:** Madrid has a lively jazz scene, and many bars have jam sessions several nights a week free of charge. The drink prices go up, so stick to wine and beer. Get there early because the tiny bars fill up fast. Try Segundo Jazz (Ⓐ C/ Comandante Zorita 8, Ⓣ 91 554 94 37, Metro: Nuevos Ministerios) or Clamores (Ⓐ C/ Albuquerque 14, Ⓣ 91 445 79 38, Ⓜ Bilbao).

4. **Make a bakery run:** Prices at bakerys are surprisingly low, and options such as the chocolate-dipped *palmeras* (heart-shaped pastries) are a Spanish specialty—and romantic to boot.

5. **Ride the Ferris wheel at Attraciones:** Maybe it's a cliché, but Ferris wheels are romantic spots—as long as you're not afraid of heights. There is a great one at Parque de Attraciones, Ⓐ Casa de Campo, Ⓣ 91 463 29 00, Ⓜ Batán

BUENOS DIAS
GOOD MORNING

11. Working

Before you get too excited about the idea of working during your time abroad, talk to an advisor in your study-abroad office to learn more about what you're in for. On the one hand, working means more money to enjoy Madrid—not an unwelcome thing, given the unfavorable exchange rate. It also presents a unique opportunity to get to know Spanish culture up close and personal.

However, working also means facing a time-consuming job search, along with a visa application process so convoluted that it will leave your head spinning. And if you do take a job, the time you spend tending bar or tutoring translates into less time to study, travel, bar-hop, see museums, and do all the other cool activities that brought you to Madrid in the first place.

JOB HUNTING

Keep your eyes open when you're looking for work: Bars and stores usually put help wanted ads (reading either *se necesita personal* or *necesitamos ayuda*) in their windows when hiring service workers. Here are other places to begin your job search:

Newspapers Start with the want ads listed in papers such as *El Mundo* (www.elmundo.es) and *El País* (www.elpais.es). The weekly papers *Segunda Mano* (www.segundamano.es) and *El Mercado de Trabajo* (www.mercadodetrabajo.es) also feature job listings, as does the English-language monthly *InMadrid* (www.in-madrid.com).

Websites Check out job search engines such as InfoJobs (www.infojobs.com), Job Pilot (www.jobpilot.net), www.primerempleo.com, and Monster.com's Spanish page (www.monster.es). There are also job listings on websites such as LoQuo (http//madrid.loquo.com) and Craigslist (http//madrid.craigslist.org).

Networking As with most job searches, networking will probably be your most effective tool. A good place to start is by finding out whether your home university has an alumni organization in Madrid. For other networking opportunities, see "Expat Resources" in Chapter 10.

TYPES OF JOBS

Your native language already makes you eminently qualified for several jobs, including teaching English, tutoring, and cafe and restaurant work. Of course, this being Madrid, the vast majority of opportunities will require adequate Spanish as well.

INTERNSHIPS

More and more, students are incorporating intern-ships into their time abroad—either during the semester or over the summer after classes end. Many students are able to balance both work and school, and an internship can be an excellent opportunity to explore a possible career path or have an extra ex-perience during your time abroad. Your university's study-abroad office is your best resource for learning more. The following websites also offer general infor-mation on overseas internships:

- **Center for Cultural Interchange** ⓦ www.cci-exchange. com
- **Global Experiences** ⓦ www.globalexperiences. com/internships
- **Global Youth Opportunity** ⓦ www.globalyouthopportunity.com
- **Institute for the International Education of Students** ⓦ www.iesabroad.org

11. WORKING

- **Intern Abroad** Ⓦ www.internabroad.com
- **International Internships** Ⓦ www.international-internships.com
- **Transitions Abroad** Ⓦ www.transitionsabroad.com/listings/work/internships/index.shtml

---

WORKING UNDER THE TABLE

Many students from abroad engage in "under-the-table" work during their time in Spain, taking on undocumented jobs such as working in a bar or cafe run by a willing owner. Though these are popular options, this kind of work setup is illegal for both the employee and employer. Even if the chances of being caught are slim, know you're taking a risk if you go this route.

TEACHING ENGLISH

Hands down, teaching English is the most popular job among young Americans living in Madrid. There are two basic employment options: public schools and private language academies. Both generally hire people who possess valid working papers, but some may offer to pay you off the books. If a school or academy offers you a position along with sponsorship, remember that a work visa takes months to process.

Colegios Madrid is teeming with bilingual schools in need of native English speakers to teach English grammar classes and a variety of other subjects. The demand for native speakers is such that most schools hire college graduates without any specific teaching degree or specialization in English. Pay varies, usually ranging between €1,200 and €1,500 a month.

Academias de idiomas (private language academies) Some academies hire full-time teachers on monthly salaries (€800 to €1,000), and some pay hourly (€12 to €20); September, before courses begin, is a good time to look for work. Many academies send teachers out to businesses, providing English courses for employees before and after work and during lunch hours. Be aware that some businesses may be located outside the city, in which case time lost commuting may not be worth the salary. Language academies to check out include the American Language Academy (www. americanlanguage.es), Club Ivy (www.clubivy.com), and International House (www.ihmadrid.com).

Programs in Teaching English as a Foreign Language (TEFL) provide lesson plans, teaching practice, and assistance in finding overseas teaching jobs. The monthlong courses can be expensive—most cost around $2,000. Enrolling in one of these month-long courses can't hurt, but keep in mind that many employers are simply looking for native English-speaking teachers and couldn't care less about their certifications. Two of the most reputable TEFL courses are the Cambridge Certificate in English Language Teaching to Adults (www.cambridgesol.org) and the Trinity Certificate in Teaching English to Speakers of Other Languages (www.trinitycollege.co.uk). For more information and a full list of courses, check out www.tefl.com.

TUTORING

Tutoring children and teenagers—especially in English language instruction—is among the easiest jobs for students to land. Many adults also contract private tutors because their jobs demand a higher level of English or they need to prepare for the English language portion of an *oposición*, an exam which must be passed to be hired for any public position. To find tutoring jobs, post fliers advertising your skills at universities, libraries, bookstores, and other places frequented by people interested in learning languages. This sort of work is always "off the books"—you won't be required to have a work visa. As a safety precaution, be sure to meet in a public place. Schools that specialize in teaching English to business people often seek private tutors as well.

AU PAIR WORK

An au pair takes care of a family's children. Typically young women, au pairs might be asked to teach English, tutor children in various subjects, and babysit. As an au pair, you can expect to work twenty-five to thirty hours per week and have two days off. In return, you'll receive a private room and board as well as a stipend of approximately €50 to €60 a week—this sum is occasionally negotiable.

Of course, your experience as an au pair will largely depend on the family you're placed with. Although most au pairs stay with their families between six months and a year, shorter and longer contracts may be negotiated. More information, including contacts of Spanish families looking for au pairs, can be found at the following websites:

- Ⓦ www.au-pair.org
- Ⓦ www.aupair-world.net
- Ⓦ www.europa-pages.com/au_pair
- Ⓦ www.greataupair.org
- Ⓦ www.iapa.org

GETTING PAPERWORK IN ORDER

The primary obstacle to working in Spain is getting legal permission to do so. Work visas, which are granted by the Spanish government and required for aboveboard jobs, are not easy to come by, and student visas do not bestow work privileges. To obtain a work visa, you must first receive a job offer from a

Spanish employer. Then your employer must initiate paperwork with the Spanish Ministry of Labor, while you do the same back at your Spanish consulate in the United States. If the Spanish government grants you a visa, you'll be legally permitted to work in Spain for a temporary or an indefinite period of time, depending on the terms of your contract.

5 THINGS ABOUT THE UNITED STATES YOU WON'T EXPECT TO MISS—BUT WILL

1. **Salads:** Spanish *ensaladas* are lacking in every way: Tuna and mayonnaise are standard ingredients, and no restaurant offers the American lunch staple of salad with grilled chicken—let alone dressing on the side.

2. **Friendly service:** Ever cringe when a clerk tells you to have a faaaaan-tastic day and draws a little smiley face on your bill? You may start to miss that enthusiastic friendliness in Madrid, where most Spanish service workers will make no attempt to conceal their disdain for you.

3. **American pharmacies:** Madrid has no equivalent to CVS or Walgreens, and neighborhood farmacias are understocked and overpriced when it comes to beauty and bath products such as makeup and toothpaste. You'll miss the wide aisles and abundant choices of home.

4. **Sweatpants and baseball caps:** No one in Madrid wears them—not even at home—and you may even receive stares from the locals if you wear either article.

5. **American TV:** You may find yourself pining for a good ole sitcom or even a vapid reality show—even though you once swore they were a waste of your time.

12. Fitness & Beauty

Traditionally, **Spaniards** haven't needed gyms because their Mediterranean diet has kept them slim and the outdoor culture has provided sufficient exercise. But recent years have seen work hours lengthen, fast-food options increase, and TV watching rise in popularity—and as a result, Madrileños are beginning to hit the gym more often.

Salaries in Madrid are low, and many people can't afford the often expensive monthly fees charged by fitness centers. Spas, yoga studios, and sports clubs, many of which are foreign owned and have English names, are typically used by the wealthiest Spaniards. Accordingly, you'll find most of them in trendy, expensive neighborhoods. Some facilities, however, such as outdoor swimming pools, are open to public use and require no membership.

GYMS AND SPORTS CLUBS

Several major sports clubs are scattered across the city center, many of them in the Salamanca neighborhood. Additionally, you'll find small neighborhood gyms with only weights and machines all over Madrid. If you're looking for aerobics classes, steam rooms, or a personal trainer, you'll need to attend the larger complexes, where typical fees can be up to €80 a month. Smaller gyms usually cost €40 to €50 a month, although all fitness centers offer discounts for three-, six-, or twelve-month memberships. If you're confident that you'll be living in the same neighborhood in Madrid for a six-month or yearlong period, your best option is to buy a multimonth voucher. Investigate these large sports clubs to find one that suits your workout needs and your budget:

Avanti Sport Center Ⓐ C/ Isaac Peral 14, Ⓣ 91 544 83 20,
Ⓦ www.avanti.turincon.com, Ⓜ Moncloa

Body Factory Ⓐ Plaza Santa Maria Soledad T. Acosta 1,
Ⓣ 91 701 04 08, Ⓦ www.bodyfactory.es, Ⓜ Callao

Centro Deportivo Narváez Ⓐ Avda. del Mediterraneo 11,
Ⓣ 91 433 32 38, Ⓜ Menendez Pelayo

Club Metropolitan Abascal Ⓐ C/ Jose Abascal 46, Ⓣ 91 451
44 66, Ⓦ www.clubmetropolitan.net, Ⓜ Gregorio Marañon

Holiday Gym Ⓐ C/ Ortega y Gasset 56, Ⓣ 91 402 44 91,
Ⓦ www.holidaygym.es, Ⓜ Lista

Reebok Sports Club Madrid Ⓐ C/ Serrano 61, Ⓣ 91 426 05 07,
Ⓦ www.reebokclub.com, Ⓜ Nuñez de Balboa

SWIMMING POOLS

You'll find outdoor swimming pools, most of which
are Olympic-size and cost €2 to €3 for a day pass,
throughout Madrid. Madrid also has an outdoor
water park as well as numerous indoor pools within
its public sports facilities (see "Public Sports Facilities"
in Chapter 13). Most new residential buildings have
community swimming pools for residents and their
guests, so if you know you'll be staying through the
summer, you might want to factor that into your
apartment search. Check out these pools:

Aquópolis Water Park Ⓐ Avda. de la Dehesa, S/N, Ⓣ 91 815
69 11, Ⓦ www.aquopolis.es

Centro Deportivo Vallecas Ⓐ C/ Arroyo del Olivar, S/N,
Ⓣ 91 303 06 08, Ⓜ Portazgo

Lago Casa de Campo Ⓐ C/ Casa de Campo, S/N, Ⓣ 91 464
46 10, Ⓜ Lago

Universidad Complutense—Centro Deportivo Zona Sur
Ⓐ Avda. Juan de Herrera, S/N, Ⓣ 91 394 11 69, Ⓜ Ciudad
Universitaria

RUNNING

Madrileños are generally not avid runners, and any
jogger you see on the streets or in parks is most likely a
foreigner—usually an American. But don't let this stop
you from taking your daily run. The city itself—with
its grand buildings and interesting sidewalk life—can
make for a scenic jog anytime, though you'll have to
tread carefully among traffic and pedestrians. The
following parks are also great places to do your miles:

Parque del Buen Retiro Madrid's most beautiful park is the
place where Madrileños go for their *paseo* (evening walk),
especially in the summer; but it's a perfect place for a run
too. The park has lovely gardens and several man-made
lakes, which make for a scenic route. There are paved paths,
but they're not solely dedicated to joggers; you'll have to
share them with roller-skaters and other park-goers.
Ⓜ Retiro

Parque del Oeste Like Retiro, Parque del Oeste has paved
paths that make comfortable running spaces; there's even
a nature route that takes you past the park's many types of
trees. Many people view the park as more "natural" than the
manicured Retiro, and you'll find fewer tourists here.
Ⓜ Moncloa

YOGA AND PILATES

Yoga's recent rise in popularity is no surprise: Eastern
influence is growing throughout the city. Pilates is
even newer to Madrid, and is quickly gaining fans.
Prices for these classes are reasonable, and most places
offer good deals for buying several classes at one time.
Investigate the following options:

Bikram Yoga An individual class is €15; a pass for ten classes, valid for two months, is €110. You can also buy unlimited classes for one month (€120), three months (€315), six months (€570), or a year (€990). Ⓐ C/ Divino Pastor 25, Ⓣ 91 523 11 41, Ⓦ www.bikramyoga.es, Ⓜ Bilbao

City Yoga Pilates classes are about €11 if you buy a set of twenty-five; yoga classes are about €7 when you buy twenty-five. Ⓐ C/ Artistas 43, Ⓣ 91 553 47 51, Ⓦ www.city-yoga.com, Ⓜ Cuatro Caminos

Estudio Lara y Miguel Angel Prices vary depending on equipment and group size; contact the studio for rates. Ⓐ C/ Magallanes 28, 1°, Ⓣ 91 594 38 63, Ⓦ www.metodopilates.com, Ⓜ Quevedo

Filpilates Individual mat classes cost €15; a private studio class using the Pilates equipment is €40. Ⓐ Avenida de Burgos 46, Ⓣ 91 767 20 10, Ⓦ www.filpilates.com, Ⓜ Begoña

Pilates Wellness and Energy Studio classes (with a maximum of five people per group) cost €130 a month, for two sessions each week. Ⓐ C/ Francisco Campos 13, Ⓣ 91 454 70 15, Ⓦ www.pilateswellnessandenergy.com, Ⓜ Cruz del Rayo

Yogaflow A month of yoga classes, one each week, costs €45. Two classes a week for one month costs €65. Ⓐ C/ Cea Bermudez 66, 5A3, Ⓣ 91 442 32 88, Ⓦ www.yogaflow.org, Ⓜ Islas Filipinas

HAIR SALONS/BARBERS

Finding a hair salon with an English-speaking stylist will be difficult; if you don't speak Spanish, you'll have to rely on gestures or photos to explain exactly what you want. Many salons and barbershops post their prices in the window. Men's haircuts cost about €10, and a standard trim for women usually costs a few euros more. Here are a few of the more popular hair-cutting chains in Madrid:

- **Jean Louis-David** Ⓦ www.jeanlouisdavid.com
- **Jofer** Ⓦ www.jofer.com
- **Marco Aldana** Ⓦ www.marcoaldany.com
- **Spejo's** Ⓦ www.spejos.es

SPAS

A visit to a spa in Madrid won't come cheap—the trip can cost €60 or more. A few select sports clubs, such as the Club Metropolitan Abascal and Reebok Sports Club Serrano (see "Gyms and Sports Clubs") have spas for members. If you want to indulge, investigate the services at these facilities:

Chí Spa An Asian-inspired spa in the center of the city that offers a wide range of services including facials (starting at €70) and massages (starting at €65 per hour) for men and women. Ⓐ C/ Conde de Aranda 6, Ⓣ 91 578 13 40, Ⓦ www.thechispa.com, Ⓜ Retiro

Medina Mayrit A combination spa, restaurant, and tea room, featuring Arab baths. A ninety-minute bath and massage costs €35.50; students pay €23. Ⓐ C/ Atocha 14, Ⓣ 90 235 33 34, Ⓦ www.medinamayrit.com, Ⓜ Sol

O2 Wellness Center Contact the center for price list. Ⓐ C/ Don Ramón de la Cruz 33, Ⓣ 91 431 40 43, Ⓦ www.o2centrowellness.com, Ⓜ Nuñez de Balboa

Sensay Integrates energizing therapies with beauty treatments, including massage, facials, and much more. Contact Sensay for prices. Ⓐ C/ Ibiza 1, Ⓣ 91 400 82 73, Ⓦ www.sensay.net, Ⓜ Ibiza

5 THINGS THAT MAKE YOU THINK, "NOW *THAT'S* MADRID."

1. **Elderly women dressed to the nines:** The elderly are highly visible in Madrid, and one of the nicest sights is the elderly women who walk down the street in pairs, arm in arm, dressed up every day as if they were going to the opera.

2. **Canine "surprises" on the sidewalks:** Despite the public announcements and signs encouraging people to clean up after their pets, hardly anyone does. For your own sake, keep your eyes open when walking on the sidewalks.

3. **Empty streets from 2:00 P.M. to 5:00 P.M.:** Many smaller stores close down for siesta in the afternoons, and Madrid's streets literally empty as people head home for lunch and, sometimes, a nap.

4. **Laundry hanging on a line:** Although Spain has made huge technological and social advances during the past forty years, most households still opt to dry their clothes in the open air.

5. **PDA:** Spaniards are notoriously passionate, and you'll see lots of public displays of affection exhibited on the streets, in subway stations, on the bus, in restaurants, and all other public places.

13. Sports

When you're stiff from studying, you'll find that Madrid offers no lack of physical activities to get your blood pumping. Public sports facilities, found throughout the city, are fairly cheap to use and boast tennis courts, swimming pools, gyms, and more. Outside the city limits, you'll find mountains perfect for hiking, skiing, and biking.

When it comes to spectator sports, there's really only one that anyone cares about: *futbol*—that is, soccer. Catch a match at the Santiago Bernabeu Stadium, home of Real Madrid, considered by some as the greatest team of the twentieth century. The city also has two excellent basketball teams, an Association of Tennis Professionals (ATP) Masters tournament, and the world's most famous bullfighting arena.

RECREATIONAL SPORTS

The dusty, arid land surrounding Madrid probably doesn't bring "outdoor sports" immediately to mind, and there's a reason for that: Temperatures in the summer are unbearably hot, sending most locals to the coastline or cooler climates elsewhere. Nonetheless, outdoor activities are available if you're inclined to seek them out during milder times of the year, and most locations are accessible by bus or train. Sometimes the Retiro and other city parks just can't compare to the real great outdoors.

HIKING

Just an hour from Madrid, in Manzanares El Real, is the Cuenca Alta del Manzanares national park, where you can see the stunning La Pedriza, a naturally formed mountain of granite. You can also escape in an hour to San Lorenzo de El Escorial, a village built around the gigantic monastery and palace of the same name. El Valle de Los Caidos (Valley of the Fallen), a memorial to those who died in the Spanish Civil War, is near San Lorenzo de El Escorial—it's marked by a gargantuan cross that's nearly 492 feet high and can be seen from miles away. Both areas are great starting points for a walk or hike.

Manzanares el Real, tourism office ⒶParque Herrén de la Boni, S/N, Manzanares El Real, Ⓣ 63 917 96 02, Ⓦwww. manzanareselreal.org, Bus724 from Plaza Castilla

San Lorenzo de El Escorial, tourism office ⒶC/ Floridablanca 10, Ⓣ91 890 15 54, Bus661 or 664 from Moncloa, Train Cercanias from Atocha

CYCLING

A 60-km cycling route that will encircle Madrid and connect several of the major parks is currently under construction; many parts of the loop are already open. Outside the city, Madrid's *sierra* (mountain terrain) is perfect for mountain biking, and many bike vendors, such as Bike Spain and Bravo Bike, organize tours in those areas (in addition to offering bicycle tours of the city itself and other areas in Spain and Europe). See "Bikes" in Chapter 3 for information about buying or renting a bike in Madrid.

Bike Spain ⒶC/ Carmen 17, 2º, Ⓣ91 522 38 99, Ⓦwww. bikespain.info, ⓂSol

Bravo Bike ⒶC/ J. Alvarez Mendizabal 19, Ⓣ91 559 55 23, Ⓦwww.bravobike.com, ⓂSol

CAMPING

Outside Madrid, there are numerous sites offering safe, forested areas for camping out with friends. These facilities maintain parking lots for cars and caravans and may include tent-rental services. Most important, they offer a variety of striking landscapes and monuments for visitors to enjoy. For specific camping information, regulations, and prices, visit the website of your intended campsite. Here are a few popular spots:

Camping Caravaning El Escorial This campground offers swimming pools, sports facilities, and even a dance club. You can also rent small bungalows. Rates: Starting at €18. Bungalows: €55 to €115 depending on the type of bungalow and time of year. ⓣ 91 890 24 12, ⓦ www.campingelescorial. com

Camping Pico de la Miel Bungalows are available for those unwilling to sleep under the stars. Rates: €5.40 per adult; €5.20 per tent. Bungalows: €52 to €126 per night depending on bungalow size and number of people. ⓣ 91 868 80 82, ⓦ www.picodelamiel.com

SKIING

While much more impressive skiing can be found at ski resorts in the Pyrenees to the northeast and in Granada to the south, Madrid's local ski options are worth exploring. Go early in the day: Valdesquí, Navacerrada, and La Pinilla, each of which is approximately an hour outside the city, are all popular winter weekend destinations. If you want a real shock, try Xanadú. Open year-round, this "mountain" is located inside an enormous shopping mall. All the places listed here offer skiing lessons and equipment rentals.

Madrid Xanadú Prices vary depending on activity and length of time; four hours of skiing access and equipment rental, for example, costs €43. Ⓐ Carretera de Extremadura, Ⓣ 90 226 30 26, Ⓦ www.madridxanadu.com

Navacerrada Prices vary; you'll pay anywhere from €13.50 to €25, depending on the type of trails you're interested in and when you go. Ⓐ La Sierra de Guadarrama, Ⓣ 91 852 14 35, Ⓦ www.puertonavacerrada.com, Train Navacerrada

La Pinilla A one-day pass is €30, excluding equipment rental fees. Ⓣ 92 155 03 04, Ⓦ www.lapinilla.es

Valdesquí A one-day lift ticket costs €33, excluding equipment rental costs. Ⓐ Puerto de Cotos, S/N, Rascafría, Madrid Ⓣ 91 852 39 41, Ⓦ www.valdesqui.es Train Estación de Cotos

IF YOU'RE FEELING ADVENTUROUS . . .

The following outdoor adventure challenges in the Madrid area will give you the adrenaline rush you've been looking for:

- **Ecoparque Aventura Amazonia** This facility outside Madrid offers rope courses, climbing walls, and Tarzanlike tightrope courses that are strung between trees. It's great for groups of friends. Ⓣ 90 251 14 62, Ⓦ www.aventura-amazonia.com

- **Paintball** Paintball can feed both your primitive and artistic sides. No Name Sport: Charges €21 for three hours. Ⓐ Paseo de la Castellana 255, 3°, Ⓣ 91 229 91 23, Ⓦ www.nonamesport.net, Bus 716 from Plaza Castilla; Paintball Park Madrid: Charges per paintball (for example, 300 balls cost €28). Ⓐ C/ V no. 3 in Las Rozas, Ⓣ 91 733 32 59, Ⓦ www.paintballpark.com

PUBLIC SPORTS FACILITIES

Madrid has a large number of *polideportivos* (public sports facilities). Amenities and entry fees vary, and you may need to make reservations in advance. For a complete list, visit www.munimadrid.es/Principal/ciudad/deportes.asp. Here are a few to check out:

Instalaciones Deportivas Canal de Isabel II Ⓐ Avda. Islas Filipinas 54, Ⓣ 91 554 51 53, Ⓜ Ríos Rosas

Polideportivo Chamartín Ⓐ Plaza del Perú, S/N, Ⓣ 91 350 12 23, Ⓜ Pío XII

Polideportivo La Chopera Ⓐ Parque del Buen Retiro, Ⓣ 91 420 11 54, Ⓜ Atocha

Polideportivo Daoiz y Velarde Ⓐ C/ Ciudad de Barcelona 162, Ⓣ 91 433 89 50, Ⓜ Pacífico

Polideportivo San Juan Bautista Ⓐ C/ Treviana, S/N, Ⓣ 91 416 42 59, Ⓜ Avenida de la Paz

SPECTATOR SPORTS

To most Spaniards, soccer is the only spectator sport that matters, and Real Madrid is the crown prince. Soccer is always big news, providing endless fodder for newspapers and magazines. Any remaining space goes to Atlético Madrid, the city's soccer stepchild, or other Spanish soccer teams, particularly Barcelona. The last few scraps go to international soccer news, cycling, and Formula One car racing.

SOCCER

Spaniards consider La Liga, the Spanish soccer league, the world's best. Matches are held on weekends during soccer season (September through May). European competitions such as the Union of European Football

Associations Champions League, which features the best club teams from across Europe, play midweek. In addition to Real Madrid and Atlético, La Liga's first division also features Getafe, a modest, low-budget squad from the southern Madrid area of the same name. If you'd like to watch soccer on television, know that most matches, even local ones, are televised on pay-per-view only, so head down to your local pub or bar to watch alongside your neighbors.

GETTING SOCCER TICKETS

The most common way to get soccer tickets is by going to the stadium's official ticket booth. Hours are posted on each team's website. Big games, such as Madrid vs. Barcelona, often sell out immediately. Ticket prices vary depending on seat location as well as on the importance of the game; they're usually between €20 and €60. On game days, scalpers often stand outside Real Madrid's stadium, although they'll likely try to rip you off. You can also try online ticket agencies such as El Corte Inglés (www.elcorte-ingles.es/entradas) or go in person to ticket vendors such as Localidades Galicia (Ⓐ Plaza del Carmen 1, Ⓣ 91 531 27 32, Ⓜ Sol).

Atlético Madrid Estadio Vicente Calderon. Ⓐ C/ de la Virgen del Puerto, Ⓣ 91 366 47 07, Ⓦ www.at-madrid.com, Ⓜ Piramides

---

Getafe Coliseum Alfonso Pérez. Ⓐ Avda. Teresa de Calcuta, S/N, Getafe (Madrid), Ⓣ 91 695 97 71, 91 695 96 43, Ⓦ www.getafecf.com, Ⓜ Los Espartales

---

Real Madrid Estadio Santiago Bernabeu. Ⓐ C/ Concha Espina 1, Ⓣ 91 398 43 00 or 90 232 43 24, Ⓦ www.realmadrid.com, Ⓜ Santiago Bernabeu

---

BASKETBALL

Basketball runs a distant second to soccer in the popularity race, but Asociación de Clubes de Baloncesto, Spain's basketball league, is one of Europe's best, and Madrid has two local teams that are fixtures in the first division: Real Madrid (yes, in addition to soccer) and Adecco Estudiantes. You can check out their games between October and May.

Adecco Estudiantes Palacio Vistalegre. Ⓐ C/ Utebo, S/N, Ⓣ 91 422 07 81, Ⓦ www.clubestudiantes.com, Ⓜ Oporto

Real Madrid Palacio de los Deportes. Ⓐ Avda de Felipe II, Ⓣ 91 258 60 16, Ⓦ www.realmadrid.com, Ⓜ Goya

TENNIS

Since 2002, Madrid has played host to one of the ATP Tour's vital Masters series events, the Mutua Madrileña Masters Madrid. The event is held mid-October in the Madrid Arena, located in the Casa de Campo park. Only the top-ranked players are invited to enter the Masters competition, and past winners of the tournament include Andre Agassi and local favorite Rafa Nadal.

Mutua Madrileña Masters Madrid Ⓐ Recinto Ferial Casa de Campo, Ⓣ 90 218 36 47, Ⓦ www.tennis-masters-madrid.com, Ⓜ Casa de Campo

5 AFFORDABLE DAY TRIPS

1. **Aranjuez:** A former royal summer vacation spot, Aranjuez is located along the Tajo River, which explains the lush and extensive parks and gardens that characterize the area. Bus from Estación Sur; Train See www.renfe.es for schedule and fares.

2. **Chinchón:** This traditional Castillian town is a popular lunch destination for both Madrileños and tourists. They come for traditional dishes, such as roast suckling pig and charcoaled meats, as well as for the local after-dinner *liquor anís* (a licorice-flavored spirit). Bus from Plaza Conde de Casal

3. **San Lorenzo de El Escorial:** The main attraction in this small town is a gigantic monastery and palace called El Escorial. It was designed by Philipe II in the sixteenth century and is more like a town than a palace. Bus 661 or 664 from Moncloa; Train Cercanías from Atocha

4. **Segovia:** The Alcazar, a castle straight out of a fairy tale, is just one of the many reasons to visit Segovia. The city also has the world's best-preserved Roman aqueducts, which date back 2,000 years. Bus from Paseo de Buses; Train See www.renfe.es for schedule and fares.

5. **Toledo:** Spain's capital until the sixteenth century, the city sits on top of a rocky mini-mountain and has an impressive royal palace and a cathedral—not to mention delicious marzipan, a Toledo specialty. Bus from Estación Sur; Train See www.renfe.es for schedule and fares.

14. Cultural Activities

The arts are one of the biggest allures of Madrid. The works of Spanish painters Velázquez, Goya, and El Greco are proudly displayed in Madrid's museums, while more modern artists such as homegrown playwright Federico García Lorca and painters Salvador Dalí and Pablo Picasso remain as celebrated as if they were still alive. Today, Madrid is becoming an important film center, and Spanish films have taken home a number of Oscars in recent years due to the international prominence of directors such as Pedro Almodóvar and Alejandro Amenábar.

In addition to its three world-famous art museums, Madrid has a rich selection of theater, film, dance, opera, and architecture. There are also countless, wholly unique Spanish festivals and traditions that will enrich your time here. Bullfighting tops the list, of course, but if bloody spectacles aren't your thing, sample Madrid's flamenco dances and outdoor fairs. You have to try hard to be bored in Madrid! To find out what's happening in Madrid every day of the week, buy the *Guía del Ocio* (www.guiadelocio.es) at any kiosk.

ART MUSEUMS

Sometimes referred to as the "golden triangle," Madrid's three most famous museums—the Prado, Reina Sofía, and Thyssen-Bornemisza—are all located within a stone's throw of one another on or just off the Paseo del Prado. These collections of mostly European art are renowned not only in Spain and the rest of Europe, but across the globe. Discounted tickets to museums are generally available for students and young people, and admission is often free on Sundays. Here are some of the "must-see" options; you can find a comprehensive list of museums and galleries at the government-run website for the city of Madrid, www.munimadrid.es:

Centro de Arte Reina Sofía Those who find the Prado's religious paintings commissioned by royalty to be a bit overwhelming should try the Reina Sofía, which is dedicated to twentieth-century Spanish artists, such as Juan Gris, Salvador Dalí, Joan Miró, and Pablo Picasso. *Guernica*, Picasso's wall-sized masterpiece depicting the German bombing of the Basque town of the same name, is a must-see. **Admission:** €6 adults; €3 students; free admission 2:30 P.M. to 9:00 P.M. Saturday and 10:00 A.M. to 2:30 P.M. Sunday. **Hours:** 10:00 A.M. to 9:00 P.M. Monday and Wednesday through Saturday; 10:00 A.M. to 2:30 P.M. Sunday; closed Tuesdays, January 1 and 6, May 1 and 15, November 9, and December 24, 25, and 31. Ⓐ C/ Santa Isabel 52, Ⓣ 14 67 5062, Ⓦ www.museoreinasofia.es, Ⓜ Atocha

The Prado The Prado Museum boasts more than 7,000 paintings by some of the best European artists. Works of Italian masters Rafael and Botticelli and Flemish painter Paul Rubens are on display, but the primary focus of most first-time visitors is the work of Spanish legends Velázquez, Goya, and El Greco. Don't miss Velázquez's *Las Meninas*, perhaps the museum's most famous work. **Admission:** €6 adults; €3 students; free admission 9:00 A.M. to 7:00 P.M. Sunday. **Hours:** 9:00 A.M. to 8:00 P.M.; Tuesday through Sunday and holidays (except those falling on Mondays) and 9:00 A.M. to 2:00 P.M. December 24 and 31 and January 6; closed Mondays, January 1, May 1, Easter Friday, and December 25. Ⓐ Paseo del Prado, S/N, Ⓣ 91 330 28 00, Ⓦ www.museoprado.es, Ⓜ Atocha, Banco de España

Museo Lázaro Galdiano This eclectic assortment of paintings, drawings, jewelry, ivory, ceramic, sculptures, weapons, and rare objects comes from the private collection of Don José Lázaro Galdiano, a Spanish businessman who died in 1947. The paintings are by Spanish and other European artists. Goya's engravings are among the museum's highlights. **Admission:** €4 adults; €3 students. **Hours:** 10:00 A.M. to 4:30 P.M Sunday through Monday and Wednesday through Saturday; closed Tuesdays. Ⓐ C/ Serrano 122, Ⓣ 91 561 60 84, Ⓦ www.flg.es, Ⓜ Gregorio Marañon

Museo Sorolla Located in the former home of the Spanish painter Joaquín Sorolla Bastida, this museum displays Sorolla's private collection. Standout pieces include not only the work of the artist but also the jewelry, sculptures, and ceramic objects he collected throughout his life and career. **Admission:** €2.40 adults; €1.20 students; free Sunday. **Hours:** 9:30 A.M. to 3:00 P.M. Tuesday through Saturday and 10:00 A.M. to 3:00 P.M. Sunday and holidays. Closed Mondays; January 1; May 1; December 24, 25, and 31; and two local holidays per year. Ⓐ C/ General Martinez Campos 17, Ⓣ 91 310 15 84, Ⓦ museosorolla.mcu.es, Ⓜ Iglesia

Museo Thyssen-Bornemisza Caravaggio, Rembrandt, Memling, Goya, Picasso, Kandinsky, and Kirchner are just a few of the familiar names whose work is on display, as well as American artists Winslow Homer, Jackson Pollack, and Roy Lichtenstein, among others. **Admission:** €6 adults; €4 students. **Hours:** 10:00 A.M. to 7:00 P.M.; Tuesday through Sunday and 10:00 A.M. to 3:00 P.M. December 24 and 31; closed Mondays, January 1, May 1, and December 25. Ⓐ Paseo del Prado 8, Ⓣ 91 369 01 51, Ⓦ www.museothyssen.org, Ⓜ Atocha, Banco de España

GUIDED SIGHTSEEING TOURS

Madrid is a city that begs to be wandered—whether you have a purpose or just want to take in the sights—and there's no substitute for exploring the city on your own. However, a guided tour can provide a good overview of Madrid and its surrounding areas, albeit at fairly high prices. If you have guests in town or simply want something different to do on the weekend, consider one of these options:

Viator Viator runs a variety of tours, such as the one-day Panoramic Madrid City Sightseeing Tour (starting at $20) and a half-day tour of El Escorial and the Valley of the Fallen, where Francisco Franco is buried (starting at $50). It also operates the red double-decker Madrid Vision buses, which allow ticket-holders to hop on and off as they please (starting at $17). All tours feature bilingual (English/Spanish) guides. Prices are listed in dollars on the Viator website. Ⓦ www.viator.com

Patronato Municipal de Turismo Madrid's municipal tourism office offers very inexpensive walking tours on a variety of subjects with English-speaking guides available. Tours start at around €3, and there are discounts for people younger than twenty-five, as well as for students.

For information on available tours and schedules, visit any tourist office (there's a central office in Plaza Mayor).

Independent walking tours If you feel like venturing out on your own, check out the walking tours detailed on the website of the Madrid Chamber of Commerce (search for "Rutas Culturales"). The tours focus on topics such as literary Madrid and medieval Madrid. All maps and route information are available as downloadable PDFs. All information is in Spanish, but abbreviated English versions are available as well. Ⓦ www.descubremadrid.com

---

MULTIMEDIA CULTURAL CENTERS

La Casa Encendida and Círculo de Bellas Artes are two cultural centers that offer revolving exhibitions in photography, video, and film. Check out the roof of La Casa Encendida, especially on a sunny day; the Circulo de Bellas Artes features one of the best cafes in town.

La Casa Encendida Ⓐ Ronda Valencia 2, Ⓣ 90 243 03 22, Ⓦ www.lacasaencendida.com, Ⓜ Atocha, Embajadores

Círculo de Bellas Artes Ⓐ C/ Marques de Casa Riera 2, Ⓣ 91 521 49 31, Ⓦ www.circulobellasartes. com, Ⓜ Sevilla

PERFORMING ARTS

The generally theatrical nature of Spain shines through in Madrid's wide offering of performing arts. Whether you're looking for the truly Spanish flamenco or zarzuela, first-rate ballet or opera, or familiar theatrical favorites such as *Phantom of the Opera*, you'll have your choice in Madrid. Best of all, hitting a show won't break the bank: You can get tickets for most performing arts events for around €25 or less. If you're looking to get super-cheap tickets, ask whether there are any student discounts when you buy tickets.

> ### SPECTATOR'S DAY
>
> It may be known as "hump day" in America, but in Madrid, theatergoers call Wednesday *dia del espectador*, or specator's day. On Wednesdays, film and theater tickets citywide can be purchased for as much as 50 percent off. Inquire for details at individual theaters.

OPERA

The central and most grandiose place to see opera in Madrid is the Teatro Real. One of the world's most famous opera houses, Teatro Real has had a turbulent history, suffering numerous fires and undergoing several restorations since the first stones were laid in 1818. Today, the theater includes a restaurant and cafe, and guided tours are available daily. You can get opera tickets by calling 90 224 48 48 (the theater's ticket sales line), going to the theater's box office in Plaza del Oriente, or visiting ticket vendors around the city, such as the Localidades Galicia (91 531 27 32). Discounts of up to 60 percent are available at the box office if you're younger than twenty-six, and last-minute sales may drop to a 90 percent discount ninety minutes before showtime.

Teatro Real Ⓐ Plaza Isabel II, S/N, Ⓣ 91 516 06 00, Ⓦ www. teatro-real.com, Ⓜ Opera

DANCE

If you're a dance fan, you'll find numerous theaters that offer ballet as well as other styles of dance.

Don't miss the experience of seeing *zarzuela*, which are part-sung, part-spoken, part-danced dramatic productions. The horseshoe-shaped Teatro de la Zarzuela also sometimes hosts the Ballet Nacional de España, Spain's national ballet company. Centro Cultural de la Villa is another excellent place to take in a variety of performances, including dance, interactive exhibitions, and theater. Those younger than thirty can get a 30 percent discount on tickets at the Teatro de la Zarzuela.

Centro Cultural de la Villa Ⓐ Plaza de Colón, Ⓣ 91 575 60 80,
Ⓦ www.esmadrid.com/ccvilla/jsp/index.jsp, Ⓜ Colón

Teatro de la Zarzuela Ⓐ C/ Jovellanos 4, Ⓣ 91 524 54 00,
Ⓦ teatrodelazarzuela.mcu.es, Ⓜ Sevilla

THEATER

Madrid's Gran Vía plays the role of New York City's Broadway, with many elegant theaters located within a few blocks of one another. Some of these theaters have been converted into cinemas, although they still have vaulted ceilings, mezzanines, and old-time theater charm. Keep in mind that nearly all theatrical productions, including those with names you'll recognize from home, are performed in Spanish. For more alternative and cutting-edge productions, you can check out some of Madrid's smaller venues. Teatro Alfil falls somewhere between commercial and vanguard, offering a variety of new works. On a smaller scale, there's Sala Triángulo, a platform for young artists to perform politically and socially motivated works. If you become a member of Teatro Alfil (which you can do by filling out a form at www.teatroalfil.com and paying a fee of €85), you'll get a 50 percent discount at the bar and one ticket to every event held during a one-year period.

Sala Triángulo Ⓐ C/ Zurita 20, Ⓣ 91 530 68 91, Ⓦ www. teatrotriangulo.com, Ⓜ Antón Martín

Teatro Alfil Ⓐ C/ del Pez 10, Ⓣ 91 521 45 41, Ⓦ www. teatroalfil.com, Ⓜ Noviciado

---

ENGLISH-LANGUAGE THEATER

Got a thirst for theater but want to leave your Spanish dictionary at home for a change? The Madrid Players are an English-language theater group that performs works ranging from Shakespeare to original plays written by company members. Its annual Christmas show is always the year's most important production. Go to www.madridplayers. org for further details.

FLAMENCO

While its capital is indisputably Andalucía, the unique hand-clapping, guitar-accompanied dance and song production known as flamenco can certainly be seen in Madrid. A number of venues, such as Corral de la Morería and Torres Bermejas, offer extravagant shows accompanied by dinner. Other flamenco locales, such as Casa Patas and Café de Chinitas, offer a somewhat more toned-down, authentic spectacle. These have a dinner option, but it's not required, which makes for a cheaper evening. For the ultimate budget option, you'll sometimes witness unrehearsed, impromptu shows in bars, such as Candela and La Soleá, where flamenco performers are frequent visitors.

Café de Chinitas Ⓐ C/ Torijas 7, Ⓣ 91 559 51 35, Ⓦ www.chinitas.com, Ⓜ Santo Domingo

Candela Ⓐ C/ Olmo 2, Ⓣ 91 467 33 82, Ⓜ Tirso de Molina

Corral de la Morería Ⓐ C/ Morería 17, Ⓣ 91 365 84 46, Ⓦ www.corraldelamoreria.com, Ⓜ Sol

Casa Patas Ⓐ C/ Cañizares 10, Ⓣ 91 369 04 96, Ⓜ Tirso de Molina

La Soleá Ⓐ Cava Baja 27, Ⓣ 91 366 05 34, Ⓜ La Latina

Torres Bermejas Ⓐ C/ Mesonero Romanos 11, Ⓣ 91 532 33 22, Ⓦ www.torresbermejas.com, Ⓜ Callao

CLASSICAL MUSIC

The most impressive and well-respected classical music venue in Madrid is the Auditorio Nacional de Música, which can hold more than 2,000 people. Teatro Real also offers a variety of classical performances. At La Fidula, you'll find a variety of musical concerts, including classical and jazz, for more affordable prices, usually around €6.

Auditorio Nacional de Música Ⓐ C/ Príncipe de Vergara 146, Ⓣ 91 337 01 39, Ⓦ www.auditorionacional.mcu.es, Ⓜ Cruz del Rayo

La Fidula Ⓐ C/ Huertas 57, Ⓣ 91 429 29 47, Ⓦ www.cafeconciertolafidula.com, Ⓜ Antón Martín

Teatro Real Ⓐ Plaza Isabel II, Ⓣ 91 516 06 60, Ⓦ www.teatro-real.com, Ⓜ Opera

BULLFIGHTING

The Plaza de Toros Monumental de las Ventas is the world's most prestigious bullfighting arena.

The stadium regularly fills with tourists and locals alike. While bullfighting is a world-famous Spanish tradition, the truth is that few Spaniards younger than thirty take much interest in it. The bullfighting season is inaugurated by the Fiestas de San Isidro in mid-May and runs through October. Tickets are divided into *sol* (sun) and *sombra* (shade), the latter being more desirable in summer and therefore more expensive. If you want to brave the sun, you can see a bullfight for less than €4, but for about €8, you can be more comfortable in the shade.

Plaza de Toros Monumental de Las Ventas Ⓐ C/ Alcalá 237, Ⓣ 91 356 22 00, Ⓦ www.las-ventas.com, Ⓜ Ventas

FILMS

For better or worse, Hollywood reigns supreme at the box office in Madrid, and posters for American blockbusters are ubiquitous at city bus stops. With few exceptions, all American movies are dubbed into Spanish for their widescreen releases. This is especially true for major theater chains. The saving grace for those interested in viewing films in their original language is the existence of *versión original subtitulada* (v.o.s.) theaters, which are few but centrally located. For comprehensive film listings in Madrid, check out *Guía del Ocio,* www.guiadelocio.es. V.o.s. theaters show films in their original language, with Spanish subtitles.

MOVIE THEATERS

Madrid's most beautiful and impressive cinemas are located on Gran Vía near Callao, where you can see a dubbed or Spanish-language film in grand style in a converted old playhouse. For a selection of v.o.s. theaters, head to the area around Plaza de los Cubos, right next to Plaza España. Ticket prices for all cinemas are reasonable, about €6. Most theaters peg Wednesday as el *día de espectador* (spectator's day), when tickets are discounted by 50 percent.

Cines Capitol Shows films dubbed in Spanish and Spanish-language films. Ⓐ Gran Vía 41, Ⓣ 90 233 32 31, Ⓜ Callao

Cine Doré, aka Filmoteca (v.o.s.) Shows classic and vanguard films on two screens. Ticket prices are less than €2. Ⓐ C/ Santa Isabel 3, Ⓣ 91 549 00 11, Ⓜ Antón Martín

Cines Princesa (v.o.s.) Plays a wide selection of independent international films. Ⓐ C/ Princesa 3 Ⓣ 90 222 91 22 Ⓜ Plaza de España

Pequeño Cine Estudio (v.o.s.) A small theater that shows an eclectic selection, including old films and classics. Ⓐ C/ Magallanes 1, Ⓣ 91 447 29 20, Ⓦ www.pcineestudio.com, Ⓜ Quevedo

Yelmo Cineplex Ideal (v.o.s.) Shows international films, including many American blockbusters, in their original languages. Ⓐ C/ Doctor Cortezo 6, Ⓣ 90 222 09 22, Ⓜ Tirso de Molina or Sol

FESTIVALS AND HOLIDAYS

In Spain, the word *puente* (bridge) refers to the tendency to maximize time off from work by turning weekends into four-day mini-vacations whenever national or citywide holidays fall on a Tuesday or Thursday. Madrileños take any excuse to celebrate, and it may feel like not a month passes without a festival in some corner of the city. Here is a sample of the many holidays and festivals that dot the Spanish calendar:

Navidad (Christmas) and Los Reyes Magos (Epiphany): December 25 and January 7 Though the Spanish celebrate Christmas, they also mark Epiphany (a holiday that honors the three wise men) with additional gift giving.

Fiesta de San Antón (Feast of Saint Anthony): January 17 Saint Anthony, the patron saint of animals, is celebrated on this day by animal lovers who take their pets to the San Antón church to be blessed.

Semana Santa (Holy Week): March or April Holy Week starts on Holy Thursday and lasts throughout the Easter celebration. Southern Spain is known for its Holy Week celebrations, which include elaborate processions, but Madrid has smaller versions of the festivities.

Las Fallas (March 15–19) Las Fallas (the fires) is a festival in Valencia that combines nonstop parties with earsplitting fireworks, as well as enormous sculptures caricaturing world figures that are publicly incinerated at the festival's end.

Feria de Abril (late April) This famous weeklong *feria* (fair) in Seville, held after Easter, is a true spectacle—and best enjoyed by scoring an invitation to a local's private tent.

Fiesta de Dos de Mayo: May 2 The Plaza de Dos de Mayo, always bustling, becomes especially boisterous on the day that commemorates the rebellion in 1808 of Madrileños against Napoleon and the French occupation in the city.

Fiestas de San Isidro (Celebrations of Saint Isidro): May 15 This weeklong festival honors the patron saint of Madrid, San Isidro, and also marks the start of the bullfighting season.

Fiestas de San Fermín (July 6–14) The Pamplona Celebration of Saint Fermin is famous around the world for the running of the bulls.

Asunción (Assumption): August 15 This Catholic holiday recognizes Mary's ascension into heaven—and also makes for a good time to take a summer weekend holiday.

La Tomatina (late August) Held in the Valencian city Buñol, this festival consists of a massive one-day tomato-throwing fight.

Todos los Santos (All Saints Day): November 1 This holiday honors all of the saints of the Roman Catholic Church.

5 AFFORDABLE, TOURISTY THINGS YOU'VE *GOT* TO DO

1. **Museo del Jamón:** There are twelve of these restaurants throughout Madrid, each offering a huge selection of the finest *jamon* (ham) from all over Spain, along with other traditional tapas. With legs of ham hanging from the ceiling, there's no other dining experience quite like it in Madrid. ⓦ www.museodeljamon.com

2. **Flamenco shows:** Flamenco is unlike anything you've ever seen. Various theaters and bars host performances (see the "Flamenco" section in this chapter). Prices vary depending on venue and performer.

3. **Soccer:** Soccer is Spain's most beloved sport, and nothing beats experiencing a game firsthand—whether it's Real Madrid or an obscure local team (with cheaper ticket prices). See "Spectator Sports" in Chapter 13 for information on getting tickets.

4. **The Prado:** It's one of the world's biggest and best museums—don't leave Madrid without seeing it. With free admission on Sundays, you have no excuse. Ⓐ Paseo del Prado, S/N, ⓉⓉ 91 330 28 00, ⓦ www.museoprado.es, Ⓜ Atocha, Banco de España

5. **Palacio Real:** Nothing screams tourist destination like the national royal palace, but don't let your desire to remain under the tourist radar stop you from going. It's truly breathtaking, and admission is just €3.50 for students. Ⓐ Calle de Bailén, Ⓣ 91 454 88 00, Ⓜ Opera

MENÚ
ESPECIAL

CROQUETAS
ENSALADA MIXTA

Y   **

PAELLA CASERA: **12** €

Pan y vino...

POR CUBIE

MÍNIMO 2 PERSONAS **

15. Eating Out

Typical Spanish cooking needs no special spices or sauces—just homegrown olive oil (Spain is the world's largest olive producer), accompanied by a touch of garlic. Many Madrileños still stick to traditional Spanish food in the comfort of their own homes, but out on the town, fast food, kebabs, Chinese restaurants, and nouvelle cuisine are everywhere.

In Spain, lunch or dinner out means long drawn-out meals with multiple courses—unless you're having tapas. Sharing a few bites of various prepared foods among friends, all eating from the same plate, then getting up and going to another place for more of the same, and then another, is so ingrained in Madrileño culture that there's even a verb to describe it: *tapear*. Finally, be prepared for some late nights. No self-respecting Madrileño would even think about dinner before 10:00 P.M., and heading out to dinner even later is common.

In this chapter, we use ✅ to indicate spots where you can expect to spend €10 or less for lunch and €15 or less for dinner (main course and a glass of house beer or wine). Keep in mind that at tapas restaurants, you can control your bill by limiting how many dishes you order.

DINNER WITH FRIENDS

When it comes to a quintessential night out with friends, going for tapas is as Madrid as it gets. As a group you'll order tapas and *raciones* (larger portions), which you'll often share out of the same plates, using complimentary bread to soak up the leftover sauce. Sharing tapas is the perfect way to taste a bit of everything, and best of all, a tapas meal is only as expensive as you want it to be. Stick to the cheaper choices on the menu if you want to keep costs low.

✅ **Melo's** Offers cheap, delicious tapas in a small, unkempt space. Don't leave without tasting the salted pimientos del padron, tasty croquetas, or immense zapatilla sandwiches. Ⓐ C/ Ave María 44, Ⓣ 91 527 50 54, Ⓜ Lavapiés

✅ **El Pez Gordo** Serves a variety of unusual tapas to titillate your tapas-weary palate. It's a great place to have a bite before heading out to one of Malasaña's many bars and clubs. Ⓐ C/ del Pez 6, Ⓣ 91 522 32 08, Ⓜ Noviciado

✅ **Stop Madrid** A traditional Chueca bar that offers quality cured meats and good wine—a great place to start your night out. Ⓐ C/ Hortaleza 11, Ⓣ 91 521 88 87, Ⓜ Chueca

✅ **El Tigre** Features a rowdy atmosphere and free tapas with every beer—no wonder it's packed every night of the week. Ⓐ C/ Infantas 30, Ⓣ 91 532 00 72, Ⓜ Chueca

✅ **El Viajero** Serves a variety of good tapas, including an excellent selection of sausages (chorizo, morcilla, salchicha. On three floors—and an outdoor roof terrace. Ⓐ Plaza de la Cebada 11, Ⓣ 91 366 90 64, Ⓜ La Latina

TAPAS 101

The gold standard of tapas is *tortilla española* (Spanish potato omelette). *Patatas bravas*, or fried potatoes served in a spicy sauce or *alioli* (garlic mayonnaise) are common among those sharing a round of beers. *Croquetas* are oval-shaped balls of creamy béchamel and bits of ham or other fillings, covered in dough and fried. *Albóndigas* (Spanish meatballs) and the sometimes spicy *pimientos del padrón* (small fried green peppers) are two more elements to round out your meal. Seafood lovers will enjoy *calamares* (fried calamari) or *pulpo a la gallega* (peppery octopus), *almejas* (clams), and *mejillones* (mussels).

DINNER WITH FAMILY

When you're playing host to visiting family members, Madrid has many restaurants that feature excellent nouvelle cuisine at reasonable prices. Chueca and La Latina are the two hot spots for fashionable new restaurants. Additionally, increased immigration has led to the opening of Indian, Thai, Argentine, Brazilian, Mexican, and many other ethnic restaurants. Most accept reservations (though they're rarely necessary), while others (Bazaar, La Gloria de Montera) use the first-come, first-served principle, leading to hourlong waits.

Bazaar Offers a creative blend of excellent Asian- and Western-style food at cheap prices, in a modern, spare space looking out onto the bustling Chueca streets. On weekend nights, expect a long wait. Ⓐ C/ Libertad 21, Ⓣ 91 523 39 05, Ⓜ Chueca

La Bola Here you can find an excellent selection of grilled meats and fish. It's known as the place to try *cocido Madrileño,* a local dish consisting of chickpeas, meats, and veggies. Ⓐ C/ de la Bola 5, Ⓣ 91 547 69 30, Ⓜ Opera

✅ **Bombay Palace** Satisfies the palate of anyone craving samosas or Tandoori chicken. The restaurant's décor is traditional Indian, and the proprietors take pride in staying authentic in every way. Ⓐ C/ Ave María 26, Ⓣ 91 468 52 58, Ⓜ Lavapiés and Ⓐ C/ Fernán Gonzalez 54, Ⓣ 91 574 19 30, Ⓜ Goya

✅ **Casa Mingo** A classic Spanish/Asturian restaurant that specializes in cheap, savory roast chicken; a hearty *fabada asturiana* (stew made from sausages, onion, faba beans, pepper, and saffron); and distinctive cider from Asturias, in the north of Spain. Ⓐ Paseo de la Florida 34, Ⓣ 91 547 79 18, Ⓜ Príncipe Pío

✅ **La Gloria de Montera** Serves great fusion cuisine and good wine in a cool, modern setting. There's always a crowd, which makes for lively dining. Ⓐ C/ Caballero de Gracia 10, Ⓣ 91 523 44 07, Ⓜ Gran Vía

✓ **La Panza es Primero** A bustling, fun Mexican restaurant that's known more for its décor—which includes a lot of cool old signs—and tasty margaritas than for its food. Ⓐ C/ Libertad 33, Ⓣ 91 521 76 40, Ⓦ www.lapanzaesprimero. com, Ⓜ Chueca

✓ **Ribeiro do Miño** Specializes in delicious seafood from the shores of Galicia, in the north of Spain. The food is great, and the prices are low—which means it's often crowded. Ⓐ C/ Santa Brigida 1, Ⓣ 91 521 98 54, Ⓜ Tribunal

La Vaca Argentina A citywide chain that serves top-quality meats to Madrileños indulging their protein cravings. One of the most popular dishes is the grilled meat platter for two. Ⓐ C/ Cañas del Peral 2, Ⓣ 91 541 33 18, Ⓦ www.lavacaargentina. net, Ⓜ Opera

Zara Offers a cool Caribbean immersion, including Cuban music, fried plantains, and other Caribbean cuisine and a mellow atmosphere in which to enjoy it all. Ⓐ C/ Infantas 5, Ⓣ 91 532 20 74, Ⓜ Gran Vía

---

NO FUMAR (NO SMOKING)

The widespread popularity of smoking in Madrid can be surprising to Americans. Go out to dinner or drinks with Spanish friends, and you'll probably find yourself surrounded by smokers—in Madrid, it's just a way of life. That said, those who've been to Spain in the past may notice fewer smokers today, thanks to a new antismoking law. Unlike similar decrees passed in many U.S. cities, Spain permits bars and restaurants to decide whether they want to prohibit smoking. Most have chosen to allow it, but all schools, universities, and offices must now enforce a nonsmoking policy within their buildings.

DATE SPOTS

In Madrid, young people usually go out in groups rather than in couples. The standard night out involves heading out for tapas, then on to bars and clubs. However, if you're looking to impress a special someone and you want some private time together, you'll find the following places to be perfect get-to-know-you spots:

Arce Features excellent (but expensive) Basque food in a pleasant, hidden basement space. This is the place to go when you *really* want to impress. Ⓐ Augusto Figueroa 32, Ⓣ 91 522 59 13, Ⓜ Chueca

Café Oliver Features an ample wine list and a menagerie of Mediterranean cuisine, comfortable red banquettes, and a lot of wood, brick, and stone. Ⓐ C/ Almirante 12, Ⓣ 91 521 73 79, Ⓦ www.cafeoliver.com, Ⓜ Chueca

Ⓥ **Lateral** Offers tapas with a modern twist, including excellent *tostas* (toasted bread topped with food) such as *solomillo con cebolla caramelizada* (pork loin with caramelized onion) that sets it apart from other tapas joints. Ⓐ C/ Velazquez 57, Ⓣ 91 435 06 04, Ⓜ Velazquez; Ⓐ C/ Fuencarral 43, Ⓣ 91 531 68 77, Ⓜ Tribunal

La Musa Offers a good selection of Mediterranean dishes, tapas, and desserts, often with unconventional blends of colors and flavors. It's a sleek but casual spot, and its popularity means you may have to wait for a table. Ⓐ C/ Manuela Malasaña 18, Ⓣ 91 448 75 58, Ⓜ San Bernardo

WokCafe Serves mostly Japanese food in a trendy, avant-garde space just off Gran Vía. Its all-red interior makes it a moody, intimate place. Ⓐ C/ Infantas 44, Ⓣ 91 422 90 69, Ⓜ Chueca

VEGETARIAN

Vegans and vegetarians face major dilemmas when attempting to eat out in Madrid. Renouncing meat is considered comical and, in most cases, incomprehensible to many Spaniards. Numerous restaurants offer "vegetarian" dishes that include bits of ham, which isn't considered to be meat. Fortunately, the vegetarian movement is gaining steam in Madrid, with numerous restaurants now advertising meat-free, health-conscious, menus.

☑ **Artemisa** Offers creative spins on traditional Spanish dishes, such as vegetarian paella, and an earthy, eco-friendly vibe. Ⓐ C/ Tres Cruces 4, Ⓣ 91 521 87 21, Ⓜ Sol

---

☑ **La Biotika** Serves macrobiotic veggie dishes, and everything from the bread to the salads to the soups is made fresh. Ⓐ C/ Amor de Dios 3, Ⓣ 91 429 07 80, Ⓜ Antón Martín

---

El Estragón Innovative veggie dishes such as soy meatballs are the specialty here. Two bonuses: meat-friendly tapas at the bar for your carnivore friends and free Internet access. Ⓐ Plaza de la Paja 10, Ⓣ 91 365 89 82, Ⓜ La Latina

---

☑ **Isla del Tesoro** Specializes in imaginative veggie dishes, with a daily menu that takes its culinary inspiration from an ever-rotating list of countries. Ⓐ C/ Manuela Malasaña 3, Ⓣ 91 593 14 40, Ⓜ Bilbao

---

☑ **El Restaurante Vegetariano** Offers a simple, basic menu and cheap salad bar for a no-nonsense veggie meal. Ⓐ C/ Marqués de Santa Ana 34, Ⓣ 91 532 09 27, Ⓜ Noviciado

---

LATE-NIGHT FOOD

Despite Madrid's all-night party atmosphere, you're out of luck if you need a snack after a late night out. Twenty-four-hour places where you can sit down with your friends are few and far between. Some kebab restaurants stay open until 2:00 A.M., as do some of the restaurants in the VIPS chain. Otherwise, you might just have to stay out a little longer—and have a snack when the breakfast places open up.

LUNCH/FOOD TO GO

For a sizeable metropolis, Madrid is lacking in the fast-food department. Sure, there are plenty of

McDonald's, Burger Kings, and Subways, as well as Spanish sandwich chains Rodilla and Pans & Company, but there is little else in the prepared, take-away department. Two chains to try are Delina's and Doner Kebab. For other quick lunch options, try one of Madrid's restaurant chains, such as VIPS, FresCo, and Topolino, which are experiencing rapid growth around the city. Find the nearest location of these and other chains by using the *localizador* (finder) option on their websites.

✓ **Cien Montaditos** Features 100 varieties of small sandwiches served with potato chips—like a real American lunch!—and cost €1 each. Ⓦ www.cerveceria100montaditos.com

✓ **Delina's** A deli-type restaurant that offers prepared gourmet sandwiches and a salad bar—a great stop for a quick lunch. Ⓐ Gran Vía 51, Ⓣ 91 559 69 64, Ⓜ Callao; Ⓐ Paseo de la Castellana 4, Ⓣ 91 576 61 32, Ⓜ Colón; Ⓐ C/ Jorge Juan 21, Ⓣ 91 576 91 21, Ⓜ Príncipe de Vergara

✓ **Doner Kebab** Offers cheap kebabs and other Turkish and Middle-Eastern food in small storefront locations all over town. They're not luxurious by any means, but the food is tasty and filling. (They're all over Madrid; just keep your eye out for them).

✓ **FrescCo** Features an immense, all-you-can-eat salad bar, along with unlimited hot dishes, soups, pizzas, ice cream, coffee, and fresh fruit. Ⓦ www.frescco.com

Foster's Hollywood Serves T.G.I. Friday's–type food, including burgers and fries, to an American-food-loving crowd. Ⓦ www.fostershollywood.es

✓ **Gino's** Offers basic, cheap pizza and pasta, as well as a set menu for lunch, in a Tuscany-inspired atmosphere. This should amply satisfy any afternoon carb cravings. Ⓦ www.clubvips.com

✓ **VIPS** Features hearty burgers, quesadillas, salads, and great desserts—a perfect place to go if you need a break from Spanish food. Try the *tortitas* (pancakes), a no-fail comfort food. Ⓦ www.clubvips.com

The Wok Features an excellent variety of Asian dishes—often difficult to find in Madrid—at reasonable prices in a modern, sleek environment. Ⓦ www.clubvips.com

---

TIPPING IN RESTAURANTS

Tips are usually optional in Spanish restaurants, especially if among young people, although servers at high-class places may expect them. Many college-age Europeans leave no tip at all or round up to the nearest euro, even when service has been good. But don't expect much in the way of service; you may need to track down your server just to get him or her to take your order.

COFFEE AND TEA

Coffee drinking is wildly popular in Madrid, and almost every restaurant serves well-made espresso drinks. Similarly, a standard Earl Grey or green tea can be had just about anywhere, but international, creative blends served with trays of brown sugar and cinnamon are available only in special *teterías* (tea shops).

15. EATING OUT

Bomec A cozy tea salon that offers a huge selection of teas from around the world, as well as all the tea products you'll need to brew your favorite blend at home. The tea salon is dimly lit and incredibly cozy. Ⓐ C/ San Joaquin 8, Ⓣ 91 531 16 15, Ⓜ Tribunal

Café Acuarela Offers tea in the daytime and alcohol at night, along with intimate lighting and eccentric décor. Ⓐ C/ Gravina 8, T 91 532 87 35, M Chueca

Delic Features fantastic desserts, coffee, and drinks in the Plaza de la Paja. Ⓐ Costanilla de San Andrés 14, Ⓣ 91 364 54 50, Ⓜ La Latina

Faborit This Starbucks competitor offers excellent coffees and shakes and also has a salad bar for lunch, a wide selection of free newspapers, and wireless Internet after 4:00 P.M. Ⓐ C/ Alcalá 21, Ⓣ 91 521 86 16, Ⓦ www.faborit. com, Ⓜ Sevilla

Gran Café de Gijón A legendary literary cafe that dates back to 1888. It's a perfect spot for coffee, a glass of wine, or a cocktail, and it also serves food (though it's on the pricey side). Ⓐ Paseo de Recoletos 21, Ⓣ 91 521 54 25, Ⓜ Banco de España

El Jardin Secreto Features a great selection of teas, juices, and coffee drinks in a tropical atmosphere—the "Secret Garden." Ⓐ C/ Conde Duque 2, Ⓣ 91 364 54 50, Ⓜ Plaza de España

Mendocino Café An unassuming neighborhood cafe that offers a book exchange/loan service as well as free board games to play while you sip your coffee or tea. Ⓐ C/ Limón 11, Ⓣ 91 542 91 30, Ⓜ Noviciado

5 *ALMOST* FREE WAYS TO SPEND TIME WITH FRIENDS

1. **Retiro:** Grab a blanket and a group of friends and head to the park for an al fresco midday meal. Pick up provisions at the grocery store or buy sandwiches at a bakery or delicatessen. Get a bottle of wine, too—it's legal to drink outside in Spain. Ⓜ Retiro

2. **Spectator's day:** Movie tickets are half-price (about €3) on Wednesdays, which is called Dia de Espactodores in Madrid.

3. **Sangria:** The Spanish consider sangria a party punch, and it's most often served in *jarras* (pitchers) that are meant to be shared by a group at restaurants or bars. The best place for sangria is the famed Cuevas de Sesamo. It's always somebody's birthday at Sesamo, where the atmosphere is always rowdy. Ⓐ C/Principe 7, ⓣ 91 429 65 24, Ⓜ Sevilla

4. **Bowling:** Since opening in 1979, the bowling ally at Charmatín has been a top destination. With twenty lanes and a full bar/cafe, it's a fun and cheap alternative to Madrid's bar and nightclub scene. Ⓐ C/ Augustín de Foxá 26, ⓣ 91 315 71 19, Ⓜ Chamartín

5. **Botellón:** In Madrid, police turn a blind eye to the young people who gather on the streets to drink, play music, and socialize in the warm months. These gatherings, called *botellón,* take place in the Argüelles/Moncloa neighborhoods near Universidad Complutense, due to the number of students, but you can find them happening in other parts of the city too.

16. Night Life

Night life in the Spanish capital is more vibrant and lively than just about anywhere else in the world. Tapas bars are full most weeknights, and you can often see toddlers out with their parents past midnight.

Weekends, which unofficially start on Thursdays, go into overdrive. Imagine taking an hourlong nap at 11:00 P.M., then waking up, visiting a few bars, settling in at a *discoteca* (nightclub) around 3:00 A.M. when the bars are closing, and finally returning home at sunrise. And imagine not finding a vacant taxi at 5:00 A.M. because the streets are still packed! That's what Madrileños call *la marcha,* and it's an all-too-common weekend schedule. But don't worry: Waking up at noon on Saturday or Sunday will still leave you hours before lunch.

BARS

Years ago, Spaniards favored bars that offered good wine and fresh beer and paid little attention to decor. Today, young Madrileños demand quality both inside and out. Bars in caves, Arabic designs, and big-name DJs are integral parts of the nighttime scene. A variety of options exist for those with stylistic and musical tastes of all kinds. In Madrid, bars do not charge a cover.

Areia Offers a relaxing atmosphere with comfortable couches, beds, a DJ, dancing, and a trendy, cool, and beautiful clientele. Ⓐ C/ Hortaleza 92, Ⓣ 91 310 03 07, Ⓜ Alonso Martínez

Bonanno A hot spot popular with young professionals who start their cocktail-drinking early. It offers some delicious tapas too. Ⓐ Plaza del Humilladero 4, Ⓣ 91 366 68 86, Ⓜ La Latina

Café La Palma Hosts live local bands performing salsa, samba, and acid jazz in its back room and gets a young, hip crowd by the bar. The myriad spaces—from the performance spaces to cafe-type rooms with tables—offer something for everyone. Ⓐ C/ la Palma 62, Ⓣ 91 522 50 31, Ⓦ www.cafelapalma.com, Ⓜ Noviciado

Cuevas de Sésamo An underground "cave" that's famous for its pitchers of sangria. You'll be drinking in good company: At one time, it was Hemingway's haunt. Ⓐ C/ Príncipe 7, Ⓣ 91 429 65 24, Ⓜ Sevilla

Geographic Club A three-floor, safari-themed bar and restaurant that features an excellent happy hour. Ⓐ C/ Alcalá 141, Ⓣ 91 578 08 62, Ⓜ Goya

Jazz Bar A small but cozy bar that plays good jazz and doesn't get too crowded—perfect for a more mellow night. Ⓐ C/ Moratín 35, Ⓣ 91 429 70 31, Ⓜ Antón Martín

Museo Chicote A trendy cocktail lounge that's popular with celebrities and other members of Madrid's beautiful "it" crowd (and was also once one of Hemingway's stomping grounds). It has a fashionable gay scene and in-house DJ. Ⓐ Gran Vía 12, Ⓣ 91 532 67 37, Ⓜ Gran Vía

La Taberna Chica A narrow tavern that serves tapas and cocktails in a cozy atmosphere. Free Spanish classes accompany your drink order on Monday and Tuesday nights. Ⓐ Costanilla de San Pedro 7, Ⓣ 91 364 53 48, Ⓜ La Latina

La Vía Láctea A laid-back, bohemian institution in Malasaña that plays a variety of loud music, from grunge to rock. Ⓐ C/ Velarde 18, Ⓣ 91 446 75 81, Ⓜ Tribunal

Tupperware Offers two levels of purely kitsch décor, including a lot of 1980s memorabilia. DJs play a mix of indie rock for a dance-loving, late-night crowd. Ⓐ Corredera Alta de San Pedro 26 Ⓜ Tribunal

TIPPING IN BARS

Tipping your bartender is optional. Of course, tips are always appreciated, and a small token—a euro or two—could serve the all-important purpose of getting on the bartender's good side in a crowded bar or pub.

CLUBS

When the bars shut their doors at 2:00 or 3:00 A.M., it's time to go to the discotecas. Nearly all big clubs charge a cover, which may be €12 or more, but a drink is usually included in the fee. There are discounts for arriving early (before 1:00 A.M.) and for just being yourself—if you're female. You can also find discount coupons in bars, cafes, and other spots around the city. Many clubs open around midnight, get busy around 2:30 A.M., and stay open until 7:00 A.M.

Ananda Offers in-house DJs, a dance floor, an outdoor terrace, and sleek Indian décor. The cover charge is high (€20), and lines to get in are generally long. Ⓐ C/ Ciudad de Barcelona 2, Ⓣ 91 506 02 56, Ⓜ Atocha

Joy Eslava Features mostly house and some Spanish pop and dance in a central location that attracts both locals and tourists. Ⓐ C/ Arenal 11, Ⓣ 91 366 37 33, Ⓦ www.joy-eslava.com, Ⓜ Sol

Kapital Offers seven levels of music and dancing, each with its own bar and type of music. It's the largest club in Madrid, and there's something for everyone, whether you're in the mood for hip-hop, house, techno, or salsa. Ⓐ C/ Atocha 125, Ⓣ 91 420 29 06, Ⓦ www.grupo-kapital.com, Ⓜ Atocha

Moma 56 A club, lounge, and restaurant that attracts a trendy crowd. The people here are beautiful and impeccably dressed—and fully aware of their elite social status. Ⓐ C/ Jose Abascal 56, Ⓣ 91 399 09 00, Ⓦ www.moma56.com, Ⓜ Gregorio Maranon

Pachá Pachá is a chain of clubs most famous for its outpost in the party-happy island of Ibiza; the Madrid location isn't quite the scene that it is in Ibiza, but it still makes for a fun night out. Ⓐ C/ Barceló 11, Ⓣ 91 446 01 37, Ⓦ www.pacha-madrid.com, Ⓜ Tribunal

Palacio Gaviria Features Thursday "exchange" nights attended by young people from across Europe and the world. It's housed inside a mid-nineteenth-century palace, so you can pretend you're royalty as you dance all night. Ⓐ C/ Arenal 9, Ⓣ 91 526 60 69, Ⓦ www.palaciogaviria.com, Ⓜ Sol

Sala El Sol Welcomes a low-maintenance, more down-to-earth crowd that's into alternative rock and electronic music. Weeknights often bring live music. Ⓐ C/ de los Jardines 3, Ⓣ 91 532 64 90, Ⓜ Gran Vía

PUBS

Madrid has its fair share of pubs, a majority of which feature English-speaking employees and clientele. These are friendly places to have a pint of Guinness, Murphy's, or other international beers on tap. Pubs are also great places to watch sporting events, such as Champions League, English League, or Italian League soccer matches. Their big screens often show NFL matches live on Sundays too. Shooters, a pub located just off Gran Vía, is also a pool hall. Pubs do not charge a cover.

Finbars Ⓐ C/ Marques de Urquijo 10, Ⓣ 01 548 37 93, Ⓦ www.finbarsmadrid.com, Ⓜ Argüelles

The Irish Rover Ⓐ Avenida de Brasil 7, Ⓣ 91 597 48 11, Ⓦ www.theirishrover.com, Ⓜ Santiago Bernabeu

The James Joyce Ⓐ C/ Alcalá 59, Ⓣ 91 575 49 01, Ⓜ Banco de España

Moore's & Co. Ⓐ C/ Barceló 1, Ⓣ 91 532 63 31, Ⓜ Tribunal

O'Connell Street Ⓐ C/ Espoz y Mina 7, Ⓣ 91 532 79 56, Ⓜ Sol

Shooters Ⓐ Gran Vía 31, Ⓣ 91 522 40 10, Ⓦ www.shooters-madrid.com, Ⓜ Gran Vía

The Triskel Tavern Ⓐ C/ San Vicente Ferrer 3, Ⓣ 91 523 27 83, Ⓜ Tribunal

DRINKING LEGALLY

Spain's national drinking age is eighteen, a rule that is hardly—if ever—enforced. High school students can order a round of beers in most bars in the city, as only nightclubs have bouncers, and even then they're primarily interested in maintaining the dress code (i.e., no sneakers or flip-flops).

LIVE MUSIC

Madrid doesn't always attract big-ticket musical acts, but you can see major acts at the recently redone Palacio de Deportes, the Palacio Vistalegre, the Plaza de Toros in Ventas, and La Riviera. On a smaller scale, Madrid has its fair share of vanguard venues, in neighborhoods such as Huertas and Malasaña, among others. A wide selection of concert tickets are available at the media megastore Fnac's ticket booth in Callao or online at www.ticktackticket.com or www.entradas.com. For comprehensive concert listings, visit www.mtv.es (for bigger shows) and www.esmadrid.com (for local acts).

Bourbon Café Features rock acts on weekend nights, drawing big crowds. Located just off the Puerta del Sol, it's a restaurant by day. Ⓐ Carrera de San Jeronimo 5, Ⓣ 91 532 58 57, Ⓦ www.thebourboncafe.net, Ⓜ Sol

Café Central A jazz club that's similar to Populart (and just up the street) and offers the same quality musicians. The music starts at 10:00 P.M. every night. Ⓐ Plaza del Angel 10, Ⓣ 91 369 41 43, Ⓜ Sol

Café Populart Showcases talented jazz musicians nightly, with no cover charge. Most shows start at 11:00 P.M., but go early to get a table. Ⓐ C/ Huertas 22, Ⓣ 91 429 84 07, Ⓦ www.populart.es, Ⓜ Antón Martín

Divino Aqualung A large concert venue that packs in a few thousand fans for pop, metal, and hard rock acts. Ⓐ Paseo de la Ermita del Santo 48, Ⓣ 91 470 24 61, Ⓜ Puerta de Angel

Palacio de Deportes de la Comunidad de Madrid A stadium that hosts arena-style groups. Ⓐ Avda. Felipe II, S/N, Ⓣ 91 258 60 16, Ⓦ www.palaciodedeportes.com, Ⓜ Goya

La Riviera Hosts huge concerts that are too big for Divino Aqualung. It's located just south of Madrid's Royal Palace and Almudena Cathedral. Ⓐ Paseo Bajo de la Virgen del Puerto, Ⓣ 91 365 24 15, Ⓜ Puerta de Angel

Sala Moby Dick Draws well-known international acts to its small, cozy stage. Ⓐ Avda. de Brasil 5, Ⓣ 91 555 76 71, Ⓦ www.mobydickclub.com, Ⓜ Santiago Bernabeu

Zanzibar An intimate, laid-back venue that hosts local artists. Ⓐ C/ Regueros 9, Ⓣ 91 319 90 64, Ⓦ www.zanzibarmadrid.com, Ⓜ Alonso Martínez

GAY/LESBIAN BARS AND CLUBS

Gay and lesbian Spaniards and foreigners head to Chueca for drinks, dinner, and dancing, but make no mistake about it—a lot of straight folk do too. Although specifically gay hangouts are mostly limited to Chueca and the surrounding areas, Madrid is generally welcoming to all, though you won't find the same level of openness—such as same-sex couples holding hands—in areas other than Chueca. For comprehensive gay listings—including night life, entertainment, and more—check out *Shanguide*, a free biweekly publication available at bars and cafes throughout Madrid.

Black & White A two-level bar that's been drawing a gay crowd for more than twenty years. Drag shows, dancing, and a glamorous atmosphere are the attractions here. A Chueca landmark, it was one of the first gay clubs in the city. Ⓐ C/ Gravina, Ⓣ 91 531 11 41, Ⓦ www.discoblack-white.net, Ⓜ Chueca

Café Figueroa A calm hangout that's perfect for a cocktail or just coffee and conversation. The old-fashioned atmosphere makes it a relaxing place to spend an afternoon. Ⓐ C/ Augusto Figueroa 17, Ⓣ 91 521 16 73, Ⓜ Chueca

Cool A club that plays house music till dawn and attracts a high-fashion, mixed crowd, welcoming everyone from drag queens to tourists. Ⓐ C/ Isabel La Catolica 6, Ⓣ 91 548 20 22, Ⓜ Callao

Pasapoga A glamorous dance club that fills up on weekend nights with an impeccably fit, well-dressed crowd. Live music is often hosted here as well. Ⓐ Gran Vía 37, Ⓣ 91 521 50 27, Ⓜ Callao

Why Not? A subterranean bar that draws a mixed crowd. Everyone's welcome here, and you'll be too busy dancing to notice the overcrowded conditions. Ⓐ C/ San Bartolomé 6, Ⓜ Chueca

OTHER ACTIVITIES

Even die-hard partyers need a break from clubbing and barhopping. Consider one of the following alternatives:

Bowling The largest and most well-known bowling alley in the city, Chamartín, is located inside the Chamartín train station. You'll even find bowling classes if you're a novice. Ⓐ C/ Agustín de Foxá, S/N (Estación de Tren de Chamartín, 1°), Ⓣ 91 315 71 19, Ⓜ Chamartín

Comedy The Giggling Guiri Comedy Club brings English-speaking (mostly British) comedians to perform stand-up in Madrid. Ⓦ www.comedyinspain.com

Karaoke Kapikas Karaoke has thousands of songs to choose from, including many in English. Ⓐ C/ Estébanez Calderón 5, Ⓣ 91 579 71 37, Ⓜ Plaza Castilla. Karaoke Marfil, located in one of Madrid's prime financial districts, has two karaoke rooms and many songs in English. Ⓐ C/ Modesto Lafuente 63, Ⓣ 91 533 48 51, Ⓜ Nuevos Ministerios

Magic La Cripta Magica (The Magic Crypt) creates an intimate environment for performers. Ⓐ C/ Tarragona 15,

① 91 539 96 96, ⓦ www.lacriptamagica.com, Ⓜ Palos de la Frontera. At Houdini, the old-time décor will place you back in another era. Ⓐ C/ García Luna 13, ① 91 416 42 74, ⓦ www.houdini-madrid.com, Ⓜ Ríos Rosas

5 COOL DRINKS YOU WON'T FIND AT YOUR COLLEGE BAR BACK HOME

1. **Calimocho:** Don't knock it till you try it—this concoction of red wine and Coke is surprisingly tasty. Some places, such as the Nike bar in Chueca, add a shot of grenadine for added flavor. Ⓐ C/ Augusto Figueroa 22, ① 91 521 07 51, Ⓜ Chueca

2. **Clara:** Half beer and half lemon soda (usually Fanta), a *clara* is the perfect accompaniment to a relaxing hour on a cafe terrace.

3. **Sangria:** Spain's most famous drink is a delicious punch of red wine, fresh fruit, and hard alcohol. Best enjoyed in a group, the most potent pitchers of sangria are at Las Cuevas de Sesamo, a famous underground bar. Ⓐ C/ Principe 7, ① 91 429 65 24, Ⓜ Sevilla

4. **Sidra:** A common option at Spanish bars, the best *sidra* (cider) is said to come from the Asturias region. Don't let its sweet, slightly bubbly taste fool you: Cider is actually stronger than most beers, so drink with caution.

5. **Tinto de verano:** "Summer red wine" is a combination of lemon soda (usually Fanta—it's a popular mixer in Spain!) and red wine. It's typically served during the warmer months of the year, but you can order it anytime.

Visas ____ Departures/Sorties

DIRECCIÓN G...G. ESTAD

-FRONTERAS-

0. 5. 92

83

ENTRAD

ENTRA

MADRID-BA

16. 9. 91

ENTRADA

BARCELONA

A BARCE

ADMITTED

U.S. CUSTOMS

778.

19 2 6

17. Going Away

One of the best things about living in Madrid is that you're ideally situated for travel all over Spain and Europe. Just a few hours of travel can take you through many countries. Spain's system of roads and trains make cross-continental travel easy and convenient—whether you're traveling to the 2,000-year-old Roman aqueduct just an hour away in Segovia or flying across the continent.

When making travel plans, consider that Madrileños like nothing more than hitting the road on weekends and holidays. The major highways often come to a standstill on Friday afternoons or before long weekends, so if you're planning to travel by bus or car, try to avoid rush hour; the roads are generally traffic-free early in the morning and late at night. The same holds true for plane and train travel, when holidays bring higher prices and crowds. Of course, when you have no other choice than traveling during the high season, book your trips in advance.

EURAIL

A Eurail pass may be the best option if you want to see many towns, cities, and countries. These popular passes cover trains and ferries and allow deeply discounted travel. Eurail passes are intended for visitors and are not generally sold in Europe, so order your pass before you leave the United States or have one sent to you from home. You can place orders directly from the Eurail website (www.eurail.com) or through an online travel service, such as STA Travel (www.statravel.com).

EURAIL OPTIONS

A basic Eurail Pass allows for unlimited travel during a specified period (ranging from fifteen days to three months) and starts at about €400 for travellers aged twenty-five and under. With this pass, you can travel within eighteen European countries, excluding Great Britain and many countries in Eastern Europe and the Balkans. You have several additional options if you can be flexible about your travel dates and destinations. Be aware that the following prices do not include additional costs for high-speed trains, certain ferry lines, and (if you choose comfort over budget) sleeping accommodations on overnight trains. Reservations are mandatory for some high-speed and overnight trains; be sure to book your travel ahead of time during busy vacation periods. You must validate your pass at the train station before boarding the first train, and you must fill in your travel dates on certain passes.

Eurail Global Pass Flexi A good choice if you intend to take sporadic trips, the Eurail Global Pass Flexi allows pass holders to travel on either ten or fifteen days (consecutive or spread apart) within a two-month period. The cost is between about €600 and €800 for youth and €700 and €940 for adults over twenty-five.

Eurail National Pass A Eurail National Pass allows unlimited travel within Spain's borders for three to ten days (consecutive or spread apart) within a two-month period.

Eurail Selectpass and Eurail Regional Pass A Eurail Selectpass allows you to travel in three, four, or five bordering countries (out of a more extensive list of twenty-two countries) for a certain number of days within two months, while a Eurail Regional Pass allows you to travel in two neighboring countries for four to ten days within a two-month period. These options can put you out anywhere from €250 to €700 or so, depending on your age and the number of travel days and countries you choose.

THE SPANISH RAIL SYSTEM

Renfe, the national train system, runs most train services in Spain. You can purchase tickets by calling (90 224 02 02) or by using the TIKNET service on Renfe's website, www.renfe.es. There are also ticket-purchasing locations throughout the city, including Renfe's central office or Atocha Station, Madrid's main artery for long-distance trains, which has its own metro stop, Atocha Renfe. Inside the station there's often an excruciatingly long wait, so take a number and be patient.

There is no single service that provides all the long-distance trains in Spain. The Cercanías trains connect Madrid with its suburbs as far as a couple of hours outside the city. AVE trains are the fastest, most modern, and most expensive. And at present, they run only to Seville and Lleida (although a route to Barcelona is in the works). Intermediate-speed providers include Altaria, Talgo, and Alaris. See "Trains" in Chapter 3 for additional information on traveling by train in Spain.

When purchasing round-trip tickets, be aware that there is usually a significant discount for the return leg: For example, a one-way ticket to Barcelona in tourist-class seats may cost €65, but round-trip tickets will cost approximately €100. Long-distance trains generally have bar cars that serve drinks, snacks, and sandwiches, and some cars have TVs that show films. In sleeper cars, expect to share your space with at least three other passengers.

Renfe (A) C/ Alcalá 44, (T) 91 562 33 33, (W) www.renfe.es, (M) Banco de España

AIR TRAVEL

The discount airline industry is flourishing, and new companies connecting Madrid with any number of European cities pop up all the time. Keep in mind that these airlines sell tickets for each leg of your trip separately, so you won't save money by purchasing a round-trip ticket. But this may work to your advantage, as it offers more flexibility in building itineraries. You can easily fly into one city, do some traveling by land, and fly back from another city without having to backtrack.

You can find out which economy airlines fly from Madrid to your destination by checking www.flylc.com, a handy site that lets you see every possible city to which you can fly from your chosen departure airport—and which discount airline will get you there. Also check out Viajar (www.viajar.com), Opodo (www.opodo.es), E-dreams (www.edreams.com), and Atrapalo (www.atrapalo.com). Iberia (www.iberia.com), Spain's major airline, offers last-minute deals on its website that are worth investigating. Here are some of the most popular discount airlines that serve Madrid:

- **Air Berlin** Ⓦ www.airberlin.de
- **Air Europa** Ⓦ www.aireuropa.com
- **Condor** Ⓦ www10.condor.com
- **EasyJet** Ⓦ www.easyjet.com
- **Germanwings** Ⓦ www.germanwings.com
- **Hapag Lloyd Express** Ⓦ www.hlf.de
- **Myair** Ⓦ www.myair.com
- **Norwegian** Ⓦ www.norwegian.no
- **Ryanair** Ⓦ www.ryanair.com
- **Spanair** Ⓦ www.spanair.com
- **Transavia** Ⓦ www.transavia.com
- **Vueling** Ⓦ www.vueling.com

UNDERSTANDING DISCOUNT FARES

Before you get too excited about that one-way flight from Madrid to London you just found online for less than €1, you should know about these catches:

- **Surcharges:** Taxes and fees can tack on an extra €20 or more per advertised fare. Some outfits will even charge you extra for booking by phone. And take note: Baggage restrictions are harsh, so check the requirements online before packing or you may face steep fees at the airport.

- **Restrictions:** Most sale fares apply exclusively to midweek travel (Tuesday through Thursday) and may involve flying at awkward times. And remember that there are usually a limited number of tickets available at discounted prices. Signing up to receive sale bulletins from airlines can give you an edge in the race for cheap seats.

- **Secondary airports:** Discount carriers often cut costs by using secondary airports, some of which are less accessible than the major airports.

PACKAGE TRIPS AND TOURS

All around Madrid, you'll see advertisements for all-inclusive package trips to sunny vacation spots such as Turkey, Tunisia, or Thailand. The prices advertised generally include airfare, hotel, and all meals and drinks, but not tax, travel insurance, and extra activities. You'll also come across ads for package tours, in which you'll travel with a guide and a group of other travelers; these tours may specialize in outdoor adventures like hiking or rafting.

While package trips and tours generally offer great deals, the destination countries tend to be inexpensive, so keep in mind that planning the trip yourself should be equally affordable—and you'll enjoy the freedom of choosing your own day-to-day activities.

Travel agencies specializing in package deals are everywhere in Madrid. Halcon Viajes (www.halcon-viajes.es), Viajes Ecuador (www.viajesecuador.es), and Viajes Marsans (www.viajesmarsans.es) are three major chains with branches all over the city. The travel agencies at El Corte Inglés (www.elcorteingles.es) stores are also very popular. One particular agency to check out is Halcon Joven, which specializes in youth travel:

Halcon Joven Ⓐ Gran Vía 54, Local 7–9, Ⓣ 91 559 71 58, Ⓜ Callao; Ⓐ C/Fernando el Católico 61 63, Ⓣ 91 544 23 53, Ⓜ Quevedo

RENTING A CAR

In Spain, you must be at least twenty-one to rent a car. Some companies will add an extra surcharge if you're younger than twenty-four; and some companies require a minimum age of twenty-five. Rental cars should run you about €200 a week, not including taxes, gas (more expensive than in the United States), and theft/collision insurance. Some major credit cards provide insurance; contact your credit card company for details. In Europe, rental cars are almost always stickshift. If you need an automatic, be sure to request it.

CAR RENTAL OPTIONS

The big names in car rentals, Hertz, Budget, Avis, and Europcar, all have branches at the Madrid airport, in train stations, and at other locations in Madrid. In addition to the major rental agencies, EasyCar (www.easycar.com), the most popular discount online rental, generally offers favorable rates. The catch is that you have to pay up front (nonrefundable), and you're required to return the car to the same place you rented it from. Carbookers (www.ebookers.es) claims to offer the best prices in Spain, and it has an English-speaking staff. Here are the main car rental agencies serving Madrid and Spain:

- **Atesa** ⊺ 90 210 01 01, Ⓦ www.atesa.es
- **Avis** ⊺ 90 213 55 31, Ⓦ www.avis.es
- **Budget** ⊺ 800-472-3325 (U.S. number), Ⓦ www.budget.com
- **Europcar** ⊺ 91 393 72 35, Ⓦ www.europcar.com
- **Hertz** ⊺ 90 240 24 05, Ⓦ www.hertz.es

You can also book a car rental through these travel websites, some of which may offer more flexibility in pickup/drop-off locations (and if you use an American site, you can pay in dollars rather than euros):

- **Atrapalo** Ⓦ www.atrapalo.com
- **E-dreams** Ⓦ www.edreams.com
- **Expedia** Ⓦ www.expedia.com
- **Last Minute** Ⓦ www.es.lastminute.com
- **Opodo** Ⓦ www.opodo.es
- **Orbitz** Ⓦ www.orbitz.com

A FEW MONEY-SAVING OPTIONS

Here are some discounts that can help you keep your expenses down on your next adventure out of Madrid:

AAA Active members of the American Automobile Association can get discounts on European hotels, restaurants, rental cars, and attractions. Ⓦ www.arceurope.com

Nomads Card Available through STA travel and online, a Nomads Adventure Card entitles you to discounts at hundreds of hostels throughout Europe as well as reduced rates for Internet access and phone cards. Ⓦ www.nomadsworld.com

VIP Backpackers Card The VIP Card will bring you discounts on bus travel, flights, activities, restaurants, and hostels. It also doubles as a rechargeable phone card. Ⓦ www.vipbackpackers.com

International Youth Hostel Association (YHA) Card You'll need a YHA membership if you want to stay at one of the thousands of Hostelling International youth hostels around Europe and the world. It also gives you reduced rates at YHA hostels in England and Wales. Ⓦ www.yha.org.uk

BUSES

Bus travel is easily the cheapest way to travel around Spain. However, it will shock no one that it's also the least convenient and comfortable of your travel options. Buses face Spain's notorious rush-hour traffic, as well as ever-present road construction and accidents. On overnight buses, expect to be woken up for mandatory rest stops, during which you'll be forced to leave the bus for an hour or two. However, despite it's shortcomings, bus travel may only cost you between €30 and €60 for a round-trip ticket that would cost twice as much by train. There are many companies that run long-distance buses across Spain:

Auto Res This line travels to Alicante, Valencia, Salamanca, Cáceres, and Zamora, among other locations. It has its own station at the Conde de Casal metro stop. ⓣ 91 551 72 00, ⓦ www.auto-res.es

Enatcar and Alsa These lines travel to Barcelona, Murcia, Zaragoza, and northern Spain. They both leave from the Estación Sur de Autobuses at the Mendez Alvaro metro stop. ⓣ 91 468 42 00, ⓦ www.alsa.es

La Sepulvedana and Larrea These buses offer service to Segovia, Guadarrama, Cercedilla, and other areas just north of Madrid, as well as to ski resorts such as Valdesquí. They leave from the same station as the Enatcar and Alsa buses. ⓣ 91 530 48 00, ⓦ www.lasepulvedana.es

Continental Auto These buses travel to San Sebastian, Bilbao, Burgos, Santander, and Pamplona, among other destinations. They leave from the transport hub at the metro stop. Ⓐ Avenida de América, ⓣ 91 745 63 00, ⓦ www. continental-auto.es

TRAVELING EUROPE BY BUS

If you're considering traveling to other countries by bus, think carefully about what your comfort and time are worth to you. Trains and discount flights are usually affordable, even for student budgets, and are almost always preferable to sitting for hours—or days—on a bus. That said, Eurolines (www.eurolines.com) offers bus service to widespread destinations across the European continent for very competitive prices; check the website for more details. Buses leave Madrid from the Estación Sur de Autobuses.

5 AFFORDABLE WAYS TO SPEND YOUR SPRING OR MIDTERM BREAK

1. **Walk the Camino de Santiago:** Spain's Christian pilgrimage, the "Way of St. James," begins in southern France and traverses Spain's entire northern border, ending in Santiago de Compostela in Galicia. Although the camino was originally a religious journey for Catholics, it has evolved into a spiritual trip for people of all faiths. If you register at a tourism office or local parish as an official *peregrino* (pilgrim), you can stay at hostels and eat at restaurants free of charge.

2. **The Semana Santa in Seville:** Every April during the week leading up to Easter, Spain throws its biggest party of the year: Semana Santa (Holy Week). Seville is at the heart of the action, with thousands of floats parading in honor of the Virgin Mary and crowds filling the streets. Be sure to book a hostel early.

3. **Morocco:** The exchange rate between euros and the Moroccan dirham is excellent, and you can try your hand at bartering at the country's amazing open-air markets—it's considered impolite if you don't.

4. **Turkey:** Istanbul was recently ranked one of Europe's top ten "under-priced and on-the-rise cities" by *USA Today*. It's one of those places you might not travel to from the United States, so take advantage of Spain's relative proximity.

5. **The Algarve region of Portugal:** Portugal's southern coast is a prime destination for tourists in search of beaches and thriving night life. Make sure to stop at Lagos, quirky home to English-speaking expats.

18. Emergencies

Your time in Madrid may mark the first time you're on your own, not to mention the first time you're experiencing life in a big city. While most students can count on the infrastructure of their study-abroad programs to assist in times of need, true emergencies require immediate action.

You should know the number to dial for a medical or legal emergency. You should also note the hospital or police department closest to where you live. When all is said and done, the type of emergency you're most likely to face is more along the lines of a stolen iPod or wallet. Nevertheless, thinking through potential "what if" scenarios in advance can prevent you from experiencing frustration and confusion when you are least prepared to handle them.

IMPORTANT PHONE NUMBERS

In you find yourself in an emergency situation during your time in Madrid, remember one number: 112. This is your all-purpose emergency number, whether you're in need of an ambulance, the police, or firefighters. 112 can be accessed from anywhere in Europe—you'll be connected to local emergency service, just like 911 does in the United States. With its English-speaking operators, this is the best choice for study-abroad students and other travelers. In this section, we'll provide Madrid's local emergency numbers. Just remember that if you call one of these numbers, you may not reach an English-speaking operator.

112 (Europewide emergency services number) Call this number from any cell phone or landline to reach medical, police, or fire services; English-speaking operators are available. Be prepared with the address of where you are, your telephone number, and, if you're calling for someone else, the victim's name and age. For more information, go to www.sos112.info.

MEDICAL EMERGENCIES

Emergency rooms at Madrid's public hospitals are notorious for long waits, and it may take a few hours, depending on the hospital and time of day, to receive attention for nonemergencies. Of course, if you have a serious problem, doctors will attend to you immediately. Private hospitals generally have more efficient emergency rooms. See the "Useful Phrases" section in the Appendix for Spanish phrases to use in the event of a medical emergency, fire, or when talking with the police.

061 Call this number from any landline or mobile phone for an ambulance. Be prepared with the address of where you are, your telephone number, and, if you're calling for someone else, the victim's name and age.

CALLING THE EMBASSY

A U.S. consular officer can assist you in the event of a medical or other emergency. Services include helping you locate appropriate medical services, contacting your family or friends, and arranging a money transfer from your bank account in the United States, if necessary. Call the American Consular Services at the U.S. Embassy at 91 587 22 40 (weekdays from 3:00 P.M. to 5:30 P.M.) or 91 587 22 00 (all other times).

FIRE

Most apartment buildings in Madrid's historic center are old, which means that escaping during a fire can be a little complicated. Many apartments are without smoke detectors or fire escapes and may be located on the interior of a wide block of apartment buildings.

Further, neighborhoods such as Lavapiés, Malasaña, and Chueca have narrow streets on which double-parked cars can completely impede all traffic.

080 Call this number to reach the fire department. Be prepared to provide a precise address or location, including floor number and door code, a telephone number, and the number and condition of any victims.

GAS LEAKS

If you suspect a gas leak, stop the use of all electricity immediately (including lights, cell phones, and landlines), close the gas key (by turning the metal lever on the pipe running to the boiler), and open as many windows as possible before calling the fire department *from outside* at 080 or 112. Follow all instructions and don't hang up until you are told to do so. If the gas is already aflame, get out of the apartment as quickly as possible and call the fire department immediately.

POLICE

Madrid's eternally packed streets inspire a sense of security, and, for the most part, the feeling of safety is well deserved. But if you do run into a problem, call the police immediately. There are three types of police forces in Spain: the *policía local* (local police), *policía nacional* (national police), and *guardia civil* (civil guard).

91 541 05 35 Call this number to reach the *Jefatura de Policía* (Police Headquarters) to report nonemergency situations, such as stolen cell phones or other petty thefts.

90 210 21 12 Call this number between 8:00 A.M. and 12:00 P.M. to report a nonemergency situation; an English-speaking operator will guide you through the process of filing a police report.

MADRID SAFETY 101

Here are some tips to help keep you safe during your time in Madrid:

- **Cafes:** Never leave phones, cameras, money, or bags out in the open—keep small items in your front pockets (never the back) and your bag in your lap. Many innocent-looking children are skilled at quickly swiping anything not nailed down.

- **Crowds:** Muggings can occur anywhere, although Lavapiés and Sol have particularly bad reputations. In crowded places, such as nightclubs, the metro, and especially El Rastro (the Sunday flea market), men should carry their wallets in their front pockets, and women should zip up their handbags and hold them tightly.

- **Blending in:** Pickpockets target tourists and foreigners, so use common sense and make sure you're not an easy target. Examining the metro map in public, shouting in English, and wearing flip-flops and shorts will make you stand out.

GETTING CITED OR ARRESTED

Spanish police have the right to carry out random identity checks, which means that you may be stopped at any place and time and asked for identification (such as your passport or residency permit). This is a rare occurrence, but make sure you have some form of identity with you at all times.

When accused of breaking the law in a foreign country, American citizens are subject to that country's legal and judicial system. This fact should not, however, inspire fear because the Spanish constitution guarantees most of the same rights and privileges (rights to due process, presumed innocence, and a fair and speedy trial) as the U.S. Constitution.

If you're arrested, the Spanish police will likely contact the U.S. Embassy in Madrid. You have the right to speak with U.S. consul, so make sure to ask police whether they've called the embassy. The consulate will send a representative, who will visit you, provide a list of local lawyers if needed, help with financial matters, and contact family and friends, anywhere in Spain within seventy-two hours. For more information, contact American Citizen Services at the U.S. Embassy.

Office of American Services Walk-in service hours are daily from 8:00 A.M. to 1:00 P.M.; call between 3:00 P.M. and 5:00 P.M. daily. After-hours emergency operators are available. Ⓐ C/ Serrano 75, Ⓣ 91 587 22 40, Ⓦ www.madrid.usembassy.gov, Ⓜ Núñez de Balboa

CALLING A LAWYER

You'll find plenty of English-speaking attorneys and law firms in Madrid. If you don't hear of a good lawyer by word of mouth, you can find listings on the U.S. Embassy's website or in the phone book.

LOST AND STOLEN PROPERTY

Lost and found offices are located all over Madrid in airports and train stations. If you're the victim of a theft, report it immediately to the police station nearest to the site where the theft occurred. Cancel all credit and bank cards as soon as possible. If your cell phone is lost or stolen, call your provider to have your service blocked.

Objetos Perdidos y Encontrados The lost and found office for the EMT (Empresa Municipal de Transportes de Madrid), which operates Madrid's network of buses. It's open daily from 8:00 A.M. to 2:00 P.M. Ⓐ C/ Cerro de la Plata 4, Ⓣ 90 250 78 50, Ⓜ Pacífico

Renfe lost and found Call here for objects lost while using the national train service. Ⓣ 91 506 69 69

Main post office Direct your inquiries about mail-related losses here. Ⓐ Plaza de Cibeles, S/N, Ⓜ Banco de España

Negociado de Objetos Perdidos This office handles lost property found all over the city, including on public transportation. It's open weekdays from 9:00 A.M. to 2:00 P.M. Ⓐ Plaza de Legazpi 7, Ⓣ 91 588 43 46, Ⓜ Legazpi

CANCELING LOST OR STOLEN CREDIT CARDS

Keep a record of your credit card details and customer service phone numbers in a safe place. Try one of these numbers in the event that your credit card is lost or stolen:

- American Express Ⓣ 91 572 03 03
- MasterCard (Global Service) Ⓣ 0800 964 767
- Visa (International Assistance Center) Ⓣ 0800 895 082

REPLACING A PASSPORT

If your passport is stolen, report the theft first to the police and then to the U.S. Embassy. To replace your passport, go in person to the passport office in the embassy's consular section (no appointment is necessary) and bring the items listed below. If you have immediate travel plans, you can get an emergency passport, which can often be issued on the same day you apply. It will be valid for a limited time, cannot be extended, and must be exchanged for a regular passport as soon as you return from your trip. If you don't expect to travel for some time, you can apply for a regular replacement passport, which you will receive in approximately two weeks. You can exchange your emergency passport for a regular passport either in Spain or in the United States.

REPLACEMENT PASSPORT CHECKLIST

Here's what you'll need to bring with you when you apply for a replacement passport:

- ✔ Completed forms DS-11 (Passport Application) and DS-64 (Statement Regarding Lost or Stolen Passport) (the forms can be downloaded at www.travel.state.gov)

- ✔ Two identical passport-size photos (photo machines are available at the consulate for a small fee)

- ✔ Proof of U.S. citizenship, if possible

- ✔ Any form of identification you have, preferably with a photograph

- ✔ Fee payment (currently $97) in cash, money order, or credit card (no checks)

UNEXPECTED TRIPS HOME

Should there be a death in your family or other crisis at home while you're abroad, airlines can sometimes assist you with securing a last-minute flight home. Each airline has its own policy on how to deal with such situations. Some may offer you a bereavement ticket with a flexible return date—however, this type of ticket is usually very expensive and often requires proof that an immediate family member has died. You can almost always find cheaper last-minute fares yourself by simply searching general travel websites like www.orbitz.com, www.expedia.com, www.opodo.es, and www.travelocity.com or by checking the major carriers with the most flights between Madrid and the United States.

- **American Airlines** ⓣ 91 305 81 74, ⓦ www.aa.com
- **Iberia** ⓣ 807 11 77 77, ⓦ www.iberia.com

IMPORTANT PHONE NUMBERS AT A GLANCE

Europewide emergency number	112
Ambulance	061
Police	112
Fire	080

Appendix

USEFUL PHRASES

Here are some of the phrases you'll need as you study, shop, get together with friends, and make your way around Madrid.

NUMBERS

Phrase	Translation	Pronunciation
0	zero	*SE-ro*
1	uno	*OO-no*
2	dos	*dos*
3	tres	*tres*
4	cuatro	*KWA-tro*
5	cinco	*SEEN-ko*
6	seis	*seyss*
7	siete	*SYET-e*
8	ocho	*O-cho*
9	nueve	*NWE-ve*
10	diez	*dyess*
11	once	*ON-se*
12	doce	*DO-se*
13	trece	*TRE-se*
14	catorce	*ka-TOR-se*
15	quince	*KEEN-se*
16	dieciséis	*dyess-ee-SEYSS*
17	diecisiete	*dyess-ee-SYET-e*
18	dieciocho	*dyess-ee-O-cho*
19	diecinueve	*dyess-ee-NWE-ve*
20	veinte	*VEYN-te*
21	veintiuno	*veyn-tee-OO-no*
22	veintidós	*veyn-tee-DOS*
30	treinta	*TREYN-ta*
40	cuarenta	*kwa-REN-ta*
50	cincuenta	*seen-KWEN-ta*
60	sesenta	*se-SEN-ta*
70	setenta	*se-TEN-ta*
80	ochenta	*o-CHEN-ta*
90	noventa	*no-VEN-ta*
100	cien	*syen*
200	doscientos	*do-SYEN-tos*
500	quinientos	*keen-YEN-tos*
1,000	mil	*meel*

100,000	cien mil	*syen meel*
1,000,000	un millón	*oon mee-YON*
first	primero	*pree-ME-ro*
second	segundo	*se-GOON-do*
third	tercero	*ter-SE-ro*
fourth	cuarto	*KWAR-toe*
fifth	quinto	*KEEN-toe*
sixth	sexto	*SEKS-toe*
seventh	séptimo	*SEP-tee-mo*
eighth	octavo	*ok-TA-vo*
ninth	noveno	*no-VE-no*
tenth	décimo	*DE-see-mo*
one-half/a half	un medio/la mitad	*oon ME-dyo/la mee-TAD*
one-third/a third	un tercio	*oon TER-syo*
one-fourth/a quarter	un cuarto	*oon KWAR-toe*

DAYS OF THE WEEK

Phrase	Translation	Pronunciation
Monday	lunes	*LOO-nes*
Tuesday	martes	*MAR-tes*
Wednesday	miércoles	*MYER-ko-les*
Thursday	jueves	*WE-ves*
Friday	viernes	*VYER-nes*
Saturday	sábado	*SA-ba-do*
Sunday	domingo	*do-MEEN-go*

MONTHS

Phrase	Translation	Pronunciation
January	enero	*e-NE-ro*
February	febrero	*fe-BRE-ro*
March	marzo	*MAR-so*
April	abril	*a-BREEL*
May	mayo	*MAI-o*
June	junio	*HOON-yo*
July	julio	*HOOL-yo*
August	agosto	*a-GO-stoe*
September	septiembre	*sep-TYEM-bre*
October	octubre	*ok-TOO-bre*
November	noviembre	*no-VYEM-bre*
December	diciembre	*dee-SYEM-bre*

EMERGENCIES & GETTING HELP

Help!
¡Socorro!
¡so-KO-ro!

Can you help me?
¿Puedes ayudarme?
¿PWE-des a-yoo-DAR-me!

Call an ambulance!
¡Llama a una ambulancia!
¡YA-ma a oo-na am-boo-LAN-sya!

Someone is hurt.
Hay un herido.
AY un er-I-do.

I need the fire department.
¡Llama los bomberos!
¡YA-ma los bom-BER-os!

I smell smoke.
Huelo humo.
Who-E-lo WHO-mo.

There's a fire in my apartment/apartment building.
Hay un incendio en mi piso.
AY un in-SEN-deeo.

Call the police!
¡Llama a la policía!
¡YA-ma a la po-lee-SEE-a!

I need to report a crime.
Queiro denunciar un delito.
KYER-o de-noon-see-AR un day-LI-to.

I was assaulted.
Me han atacado.
me an a-ta-KA-do.

I was mugged.
Me han atracado.
me an a-tra-KA-do.

I lost . . .
He perdido . . .
e per-DEE-do . . .

Someone stole . . .
Alguien ha robado . . .
al-GHYEN a ro-BA-do . . .

My wallet/purse/passport/cell phone . . .
Mi cartera/bolso/pasaporte/movil . . .
mee kar-TE-ra | BOL-so | pa-sa-POR-te | MO-vil . . .

My address is . . .
Mi dirección es . . .
mee deer-ek-si-ON es

My telephone number is . . .
Mi numero de telefono es . . .
mee NOO-mero de te-LE-fono es . . .

I am on the ___ floor.
Estoy en la ___ piso.
e-STOY en la ___ PEE-so.

GREETINGS & INTRODUCTIONS

Hello!
¡Hola!
¡O-la!

Good morning/afternoon/evening!
¡Buenos días/tardes/noches!
¡BWE-nos DEE-as|TAR-des|NO-ches!

How are you?
¿Cómo estás?
¿KO-mo es-TAS?

I'm great/not so great.
Estoy muy bien/no muy bien.
es-TOY mooy byen|no mooy byen.

What's up?
¿Qué pasa?
¿ke PA-sa?

Nothing much.
Nada.
NA-da.

What's your name?
¿Cómo te llamas?
¿KO-mo te YA-mas?

My name is . . .
Me llamo . . .
me YA-mo . . .

Pleased to meet you.
Mucho gusto.
MOO-cho GOO-stoe.

Where are you from?
¿De donde eres?
¿de DON-de ER-es?

Are you from [Madrid]?
¿Eres de [Madrid]?
¿ER-es de [ma-DRID]?

I'm from the United States.
Soy de los estados unidos.
soy de los es-TAD-os oo-NI-dos.

I'm a student at . . .
Soy estudiante de . . .
Soy estu-di-AN-te . . .

I study . . .
Estudio . . .
es-TOOD-yo . . .

Where do you live?
¿Dónde tu vives?
¿DON-de tu VEE-ves?

I live . . .
Vivo . . .
VEE-vo . . .

Is this seat/table taken?
¿Está ocupada esta silla/mesa?
¿es-TA oku-PA-da ES-ta SEE-ya/MAY-sa?

How long will you be in [Madrid]?
¿Cuanto tiempo estarás en [Madrid]?
¿KWAN-toe TEE-yempo estar-AS en [ma-DRID]?

This is my friend . . .
Este es mi amigo . . .
ES-te es mee a-MI-go . . .

Goodbye.
Adiós.
a-DYOS.

See you later/tomorrow.
Hasta luego/mañana.
A-sta LWE-go | ma-NYA-na.

GETTING CONNECTED

What's your email?
¿Cuál es tu email?
¿kwal es too EE-meil?

What's your phone number?
¿Cual es tu número de teléfono?
¿kwal es too NOO-mero de te-LE-fono?

I'll call you.
Te llamo.
te YA-mo.

Call me sometime.
Llamame algun día.
YA-ma-me al-GOON DEE-ya.

What's your address?
¿Cual es tu dirección?
¿kwal es too deer-ek-si-ON?

PLEASANTRIES

Please.
Por favor.
por fa-VOR.

Thank you.
Gracias.
GRA-syas.

You're welcome.
De nada.
de NA-da.

Excuse me.
Permiso.
per-MEE-so.

Sorry.
Lo siento.
lo SYEN-toe.

ON CAMPUS

Did you study?
¿Has estudiado?
¿AHHS estoodi-A-do?

Can I look at your notes?
¿Puedo ver tus apuntes?
¿PUAY-do ver toos ah-PUN-tays?

Want to meet after class?
¿Quieres quedar después de clase?
¿KYER-es kay-DAR des-poo-ES de CLASS-ey?

I'm going to the library.
Voy a la biblioteca.
VOY a la biblio-TAY-ka.

Can I borrow your textbook?
¿Me dejas tu libro?
¿may DAY-has too LEE-bro?

I forgot my homework.
Olvidé mis deberes.
Olvee-DAY mees day-ber-AYS.

I need an extension.
Necesito mas tiempo.
ne-se-SEE-toe mas tee-YEM-po.

What grade did you get?
¿Que nota has sacado?
¿Ke nota AHS sa-KA-do?

Do you have any idea what's going on?
¿Tienes alguna idea de que está pasando?
¿ TYEN-es al-GOO-na ee-DE-a de ke es-TA pa-SAN-do?

I need coffee.
Necesito un café.
ne-se-SEE-toe oon ca-FE.

LANGUAGE

Do you speak English?
¿Hablas inglés?
¿A-blas een-GLES?

I speak English.
Hablo ingles.
A-blo een-GLES.

I don't speak Spanish.
No hablo español.
no A-blo es-pa-NYOL.

I speak only a little Spanish.
Hablo poco español.
A-blo PO-co es-pa-NYOL.

I don't understand.
No comprendo.
no com-PREN-do.

Do you understand me?
¿Me entiendes?
¿may en-ti-YEN-dees?

Speak more slowly, please.
Habla mas despacio, por favor.
A-bla maas des-PA-seeo, por fa-VOR.

Can you repeat that, please?
¿Puedes repetir, por favor?
¿PWE-des re-pe-TIR, por fa-VOR?

DIRECTIONS & GETTING AROUND

Where is . . .
Donde esta . . .
DON-de e-STA . . .

What is the address?
¿Cual es la dirección?
¿kwal es la deer-ek-si-ON?

Left
A la izquierda
a la ees-KYER-da

Right
A la derecha
a la de-RE-cha

Across from
Enfrente de
en-FREN-te de

Next to
Al lado de
Ahl LA-dough de

Behind
Detras de
de-TRAS de

In front of
Enfrente de
en-FREN-te de

Where's the nearest metro/bus stop?
¿Dónde está la parada más cercana del metro/de autobuses?

¿DON-de e-STA la pa-RA-da mahs cer-CAN-na del ME-tro| de auto-BU-says?

Where can I catch a taxi?
¿Dónde puedo coger un taxi?
¿DON-de PWE-do co-HAIR un taxi?

SHOPPING

Open
Cerrado
cer-RA-do

Closed
Abierto
a-bee-YER-toe

Can I try it on?
¿Me lo puedo probar?
¿me lo PWE-do pro-BAR?

How much does this cost?
¿Cuánto cuesta?
¿KWAN-toe KWES-ta?

I'm just browsing.
Sólo estoy mirando.
SO-lo e-STOY mee-RAN-do.

Do you sell . . . ?
¿Venden . . . ?
¿VEN-den . . . ?

It doesn't fit me.
No me queda bueno.
no me KE-da BWE-no.

Do you have something in a larger/smaller size?
¿Tiene algo de una talla más grande/pequeña?
¿TYEN-e al-go de oo-na TA-ya mas GRAN-de|pe-KE-nya?

Do you take credit cards?
¿Se aceptan tarjetas de crédito?
¿se a-SEP-tan tar-HE-tas de KRE-dee-toe?

I'd like to buy this.
Me gustaría comprar esto.
may goose-tar-EYA com-PRAR ES-toe.

Is this returnable?
¿Se puede devolver?
¿say PWE-de de-vol-VER?

EATING OUT

Where should we eat?
¿Donde debemos comer?
¿DON-de de-BAY-mos co-MER?

Is it cheap?
¿Es barato?
¿es ba-RA-toe?

Is it nearby?
¿Está cerca?
¿e-STA SER-ka?

What kind of food do they serve?
¿Qué tipo de comida sirven?
¿ke TEE-po de ko-MEE-da SEER-ven?

Can they take a big group?
¿Pueden aceptar un grupo grande?
¿PWE-den a-sep-TAR oon GROO-po GRAN-de?

How late do they serve food?
¿Hasta qué hora sirven comida?
¿A-sta ke O-ra SEER-ven ko-MEE-da?

We'd like a table for [four].
Quisiéramos una mesa para [cuatro].
kee-SYE-ra-mos oo-na ME-sa pa-ra [KWA-tro].

I'm waiting for someone.
Estoy esperando para alguien.
e-STOY e-spe-ran-do pa-ra al-gyen.

My friends will be here soon.
Mis amigos llegarán pronto.
mees a-MEE-gos ye-ga-RAN PRON-toe.

May I see a menu?
¿Me puede dar una menú?
¿me PWE-de dar oo-na me-NOO?

I'll have . . .
Voy a pedir . . .
voy a pe-DEER . . .

The check, please.
La cuenta, por favor.
la KWEN-ta, por fa-VOR.

GOING OUT

What are you up to tonight?
¿Qué haces esta noche?
¿ke A-ses E-sta NO-che?

You feel like doing something?
¿Tienes ganas de hacer algo?
¿TYEN-es GA-nas de a-SER AL-go?

What do you feel like doing?
¿Qué quieres hacer?
¿ke KYER-es a-SER?

I'm in the mood to . . .
Tengo ganas de . . .
TEN-go GA-nas de . . .

What time do you want to meet?
¿Hasta qué hora te quieres quedar?
¿a-sta ke O-ra te KYER-es ke-DAR?

I'm running late.
Estoy atrasado.
e-STOY a-tra-SA-do.

I'm ready!
¡Estoy listo/a!
¡e-STOY LEE-sto|a!

Where do you want to meet?
¿Dónde quieres encontrarnos?
¿DON-de KYER-es en-kon-TRAR-nos?

I'll meet you there.
Te veo allí.
te VE-o a-YEE.

Do you have money?
¿Tienes dinero?
¿TYEN-es dee-NE-ro?

Are you bringing a bag?
¿Traes una bolsa?
¿TRA-es oo-na BOL-sa?

What are you going to wear?
¿Qué vas a llevar?
¿ke vas a ye-VAR?

Is there dancing?
¿Se baila?
¿se BAI-la?

Let's go somewhere else.
Vamos a otro lugar.
VA-mos a o-tro loo-GAR.

Is there an ATM around here?
¿Hay un cajero automático por aquí?
¿ai oon ka-HE-ro ow-toe-MA-tee-ko por a-KEE?

CONVERSIONS

U.S. TO METRIC

1 in	25.4 mm
1 in	2.54 cm
1 ft	0.3 m
1 sq. ft	0.09 sq. m
1 mile	1.6 km
1 lb	0.45 kg
1 lb	0.07 stone (U.K.)
1 oz	28 g
1 gallon	3.79 liters

METRIC TO U.S.

1 mm	0.039 in
1 cm	0.39 in
1 m	3.28 ft
1 sq. m	10.76 sq. ft
1 km	0.62 mile
1 kg	2.2 lb
1 stone (U.K.)	14 lb
1 g	0.04 oz
1 liter	0.26 gallons

TEMPERATURE

$C = F - 32 / 1.8$

$F = C \times 1.8 + 32$

CLOTHING SIZES

Important note: These sizes are approximate! Always try things on before you buy them. Also note that in the U.K., shoes are not always sold in half sizes, and some stores sell shoes in European or U.S. sizes.

WOMEN'S CLOTHES

U.S.	4	6	8	10	12	14
U.K.	6	8	10	12	14	16
Europe	34	36	38	40	42	44

MEN'S CLOTHES

U.S./U.K.	35	36	37	38	39	40
Europe	46	48	50	52	54	56

WOMEN'S SHOES

U.S.	5	6	7	8	9	10
U.K.	3.5	4.5	5.5	6.5	7.5	8.5
Europe	36	37	39	40	41	42

MEN'S SHOES

U.S.	7	8	9	10	11	12
U.K.	6.5	7.5	8.5	9.5	10.5	11.5
Europe	40	41	42	44	45	47

COUNTRY CODES

Here are some commonly used country codes in Western Europe and North America. Note that many European phone numbers start with a 0, which should only be used when dialing within the country.

Austria	43
Belgium	32
Canada	1
Denmark	45
Finland	358
France	33
Germany	49
Greece	30
Italy	39
Netherlands	31
Norway	47
Poland	48
Portugal	351
Republic of Ireland	353
Spain	34
Sweden	46
Switzerland	41
United Kingdom	44
United States	1

ABOUT THE WRITER

MICHAEL RAPHAN was born and raised in New York. In 2002, he graduated from Northwestern University with an expensive degree. Post-graduation, he purchased a briefcase and plodded through New York City investigating insurance claims and then shocked friends and family by moving to Spain, where he had attended college for a semester. This led him to begin teaching English as a second language. After three years in the Spanish capital, Michael moved to Hollywood to write screenplays. He's currently lamenting the move and dreaming about a triumphant return to Madrid.

PHOTO CREDITS

1. **Paperwork & Practicalities** © Carl & Ann Purcell/Corbis
2. **The Neighborhoods** © Kelvin Wakefield/iStockphoto
3. **Getting Around** © Elena Solodovnikova/Shutterstock
4. **Finding Housing** © Amparo Fontanet/Shutterstock
5. **Shopping** © Hola Images/Getty Images
6. **Daily Living** © Marcus Alkemade/iStockphoto
7. **Studying & Staying Informed** © Manuel Valesco/iStockphoto
8. **Staying in Touch** © Zina Seletskaya/Shutterstock
9. **Health** © Anthony Hall/iStockphoto
10. **Getting Involved** © Nick Dolding/Taxi/GettyImages
11. **Working** © Andreas Guskos/iStockphoto
12. **Fitness & Beauty** © Thomas Lammeyer/iStockphoto
13. **Sports** © Elena Sherengovskaya/Shutterstock
14. **Cultural Activities** © Peter Adams/Getty Images
15. **Eating Out** © Manuel Velasco/iStockphoto
16. **Night Life** © Emmanelle Morand/Paulette/Fotolia
17. **Going Away** © Gary Paul Lewis/Shutterstock
18. **Emergencies** © Hola Images/Getty Images

INDEX